A Locals' Guide
to South Carolina's Best Kept Dining Secrets

For Maggie

You will be ready in a moment's notice.

Love,
Dad & Mom
Christmas, 2005

A Locals'
Guide to
South Carolina's
Best Kept Dining Secrets

Brian
Katonak

with **Lynne**
Katonak

SANDLAPPER PUBLISHING CO., INC.
Orangeburg, South Carolina

First Edition

Published by Sandlapper Publishing Co., Inc.
Orangeburg, South Carolina

Manufactured in the United States of America

Library of Congress Cataloging-in-Publication-Data

Katonak, Brian, 1967
    A locals' guide to South Carolina's best kept dining secrets /
by Brian Katonak with Lynne Katonak. — 1st ed.
        p.   cm.
    ISBN 0-87844-146-8
    1. Restaurants—South Carolina—Guidebooks. I. Katonak, Lynne,
1936–
TX907.3.S673 K37   1999
647.95757—dc21   98-29727
                                                                              CIP

Dedicated to the
"Rainbow Girl"

~~

May your colors and light continue to shine,
as they have upon my life.—B.K.

Acknowledgement

My 1997 New Year's resolution was to start and complete this project during the year. I began compiling a list of restaurants in the spring and started visiting them during the summer. When it became obvious what a job it would be, my mother, Lynne Katonak, offered her assistance. A past winner of the South Carolina Female Journalist of the Year award, she interviews people well and knows all about deadlines. It's doubtful this book would have been finished without her help—and that of my father, Paul, who has served as her chauffeur and chief assistant for the past four decades.

Questions Frequently Asked
During the Research for This Book

What kinds of restaurants are represented?
You name it; we've got it. Some of them are inexpensive "dives" while others are sophisticated gourmet bistros. A few might be called "greasy spoons" while others are noted five-star restaurants. The sampling is extensive.

How were the restaurants chosen?
These restaurants aren't necessarily the most well publicized or famous in any area but are places where the locals are said to eat. Many are off the beaten track and therefore not readily discovered by outsiders.

Who offered recommendations on places to be included?
Anyone and everyone. We inquired of local businessmen, attorneys, housewives, construction workers, secretaries, bankers, judges, and anyone else familiar with an area.

What criteria was used in determining places to include?
The restaurant had to be locally owned and could not be part of a chain or franchise.

Were any particular kinds of restaurants disqualified from selection?
I decided not to include barbecue restaurants in this book since there are already guides available to those places.

How did you decide what places to include?
It was important that there be at least one restaurant from each county in the state. Of course, the more heavily populated counties offered a bigger selection. I tried to be as comprehensive as I could.

Questions Frequently Asked
During the Research for This Book

Did you visit every restaurant in the book?
Yes. And I've got the gas receipts to prove it. I felt it was essential to actually go to each restaurant and check it out personally and talk with the owners. There were places recommended I did not feel were suitable.

How is the book organized?
I have divided the state into five regions: Upstate, Midlands, Riverside, Pee Dee, and Coastal. The restaurants are presented by county in each region. Each review is introduced by a listing of basic information about the restaurant—owners' names, highway directions, hours of operation, availability of children's menu, availability of light or diet dishes, and other pertinent facts—for quick reference. Next, the reader will learn how the owner got into the business or hear the history of the restaurant. Concluding each section is a review of the food that is served.

How did this project come about?
I have always traveled a great deal throughout the Palmetto State and realized that almost every town has at least one special place the locals like to eat. The problem was, I often heard about these places *after* I left the area. I started thinking how great it would be if someone wrote a guidebook to local restaurants so that visitors would know about them. I finally decided that someone might as well be me.

What qualifications do you have to do this book?
I love South Carolina. I love to write. And I love to eat.

Contents

The state has been divided into five geographic regions. Restaurants are listed by county in the region in which they are located. In each case, the name of the county is followed by the restaurant's name and the city in, or near, which you will find it.

Contents (cont'd.)

A Word to the Wise (and Hungry)

As with many things in life, you often have to look hard to discover the very best kept secrets. A number of the restaurants in this book truly are *hidden* gems (in other words, they can be difficult to find). While traveling to many of these places, I often said to myself, "It can't be out here!"

In order to help each of you enjoy these wonderful restaurants I have attempted to provide as accurate direction as possible, and I have included phone numbers in case you have a problem. If you are traveling any great distance to try out one of my selections, it might be a good idea to call first to make sure they're open. Unlike the chains, many locally owned restaurants close down when the owners go on vacation.

Should you have real difficulty finding a particular restaurant, just stop in the closest town and ask. I have no doubt the locals can guide you to your destination!

Just for fun, I've added little bits of trivia about
South Carolina here and there throughout the book.

A Locals' Guide
to South Carolina's Best Kept Dining Secrets

Upstate

ABBEVILLE COUNTY
   Yoder's Dutch Kitchen (Abbeville)
ANDERSON COUNTY
   Skin Thrasher's Hot Dogs (Anderson)
   The Towne House (Anderson)
CHEROKEE COUNTY
   Brannon's Seafood (Gaffney)
GREENVILLE COUNTY
   The Fork Restaurant (Greer)
   McBees Diner (Greenville)
   Olympian (Greenville)
   The Open Hearth Greenville)
LAURENS COUNTY
   Harry's Old-Fashioned Hamburgers (Clinton)
OCONEE COUNTY
   Steak House Cafeteria (Walhalla)
PICKENS COUNTY
   Sardi's Den (Clemson)
   Villa Luigi (Central)
SPARTANBURG COUNTY
   Mimi's (Spartanburg)
   Woodward's Cafe (Spartanburg)
UNION COUNTY
   Heart Family Restaurant (Union)
YORK COUNTY
   The Coal Yard Restaurant (York)
   Ebenezer Grill (Rock Hill)

Yoder's Dutch Kitchen

Owner or manager:	Melvin Yoder
Address:	809 E. Greenwood Street, Abbeville
Directions:	From the intersection of SC 28 and SC 72, downtown Abbeville, take SC 72 (Greenwood Street) NE (toward Greenwood) approx. 2 miles. Restaurant on left side of street.
Phone number:	864-459-8047
Hours of operation:	WED–SAT 11:00am–2:30pm, 5:00–8:30pm
Payment method:	checks
Reservations:	not needed
Dress:	casual to dressy
Gratuity:	not included
Bar:	no
Alcohol:	not served
Diet/light menu:	no
Children's menu:	child's plate available
Average price for meal:	$5.75, lunch • $8.50, dinner
Discounts:	none offered
Catering:	no
House favorites:	fried chicken, shrimp, all vegetables
Other:	non-smoking, family environment

Residents of Abbeville don't need to travel to Pennsylvania to sample traditional Dutch Amish cooking. They can simply make the short drive to Yoder's, a local favorite for over twenty-seven years.

The Yoder family is actually Mennonite, not Amish. But manager Melvin Yoder explained that their religion branched off from the more familiar Amish sect. "We are pretty close in a lot of ways," he says, "though Mennonites interpret several important areas of the Bible differently. Both of my parents were originally Amish."

The Mennonite Church to which the Yoders belong was formerly located in Virginia Beach. In the late 1960s the church felt that Virginia Beach was becoming too big, so it looked around for a community that was much smaller and more conducive to their lifestyle. They chose Abbeville, South Carolina, and the members began moving to the area. The Yoder family was the fifth to relocate. In the move, Melvin left behind his job as manager of a dairy in Virginia and began looking for a business to run in his new homeplace. He almost opted for a grocery store but changed his mind at the last minute. He decided to try the restaurant business, though he had no formal training or experience.

Since its opening in December 1970, Yoder's has prospered. The restaurant does little advertising and credits its success to favorable word of mouth.

Yoder's is very much a family-oriented establishment. And though the atmosphere is casual, Melvin is appreciative that his patrons show modesty in dress. Most of the waitresses are members of the Yoders' church and wear small bonnets in honor of the Mennonite tradition. It is interesting to note that the main cook, Betty Housey, has been at the restaurant for twenty years but is herself not a Mennonite.

Melvin points out that while Yoder's does serve many Mennonite dishes, some of its most popular items, such as fried chicken, broccoli casserole, and macaroni casserole, are

southern specialties. The restaurant is open for lunch and dinner. At midday patrons are offered the mini-lunch (a meat and two vegetables, $4.95) or the regular lunch (a meat and three vegetables, $5.75).

Dinner is an all-you-can-eat buffet ($8.50)—although such large servings are given on the first pass, it is difficult to return for more. The dinner buffet offers a wide selection of meats, but it seems to me the vegetables really make this restaurant special. Cooked with traditional spices, you will find yourself devouring vegetables you haven't had since your mother made you eat them as a child. It's probably best to ask for a small taste of everything. If you want to say you had real Mennonite food, try any of the items served with cabbage. The bread and desserts are all homemade and should not be missed.

The most difficult decision at Yoder's is not *what* to select, but what *not* to select. No matter what you choose you'll come away pleased. Make sure you don't arrive too late; they quit serving new customers at 8:30 P.M.

♦ The Opera House in Abbeville, built in the early 1900s, was a place of entertainment for northerners who stopped through town on their train rides to Florida. The building was closed for years but has now been fully restored and is open once again for live theatre.

Skin Thrasher's Hot Dogs

Owner or manager:	Mike Thrasher, Matt Thrasher, Wayne Harbin
Address:	203 Hudgens Street, Anderson
Directions:	From I-85, take US 76 (exit 19) S toward Anderson. After you pass the Anderson Mall, US 76 becomes Main Street. Continue on Main for approx. 3 miles to Whitner St. (courthouse on corner). Turn left onto Whitner and go about 1-1/2 miles to Hudgens. Restaurant at corner of Whitner and Hudgens.
Phone number:	864-225-9229
Hours of operation:	TUE–SAT 11:00AM–7:00PM
Payment method:	cash only
Reservations:	not needed
Dress:	casual
Gratuity:	not included
Bar:	no
Alcohol:	beer—limit of two
Diet/light menu:	no
Children's menu:	no
Average price for meal:	85¢ per hot dog
Discounts:	none offered
Catering:	no
House favorites:	hot dogs!
Other:	two other locations in Anderson

Question: Can a restaurant in the middle of a decaying mill village serve only one item and still prosper? Answer: Of course, if that restaurant is Skin Thrasher's Hot Dogs, an Anderson tradition since 1946.

The place was a sandwich shop and pool room when it was bought by Lloyd ("Skin") Thrasher over fifty years ago. (He gained his nickname as a child after a barber gave him too short a haircut.) The shop was a central hangout in the thriving mill village in which Skin grew up, and he thought owning a restaurant was a better career choice than working in the textile industry. After taking over the place, Skin introduced hot dogs to the menu. They proved to be so popular, he had to remove the pool tables to accommodate the growing number of customers. He soon realized no one really cared about the sandwiches, so he dropped everything from the menu except the popular hot dogs.

When you enter the small building on Hudgens Street, you may at first think you have stepped back into a different era. In the center is a counter encircled by stools, and a handful of tables with chairs are scattered about. The limited seating forces customers to share whatever space is available, forming a true melting pot of Anderson society. It isn't uncommon for doctors and lawyers to share a table with mill workers and farmers. Displayed on the walls are large tin signs stating, "No Profanity, Please!" and "Two Beer Limit."

If you are hesitant about going into the restaurant once you arrive, you are not alone. Several years ago a mother visited her son who was attending college in Anderson. He had mentioned Thrasher's to her and decided to take her there. Upon arriving at the restaurant the woman refused to leave the safety of her car. When the son's pleas didn't sway her, he went inside and told Skin the problem.

The owner walked out to the car and explained to the apprehensive lady that she had nothing to worry about. When

she still refused to move, he made her a deal. "If it would make you feel better," he said, "there are two SLED agents eating now. I'll send them out and have you escorted in." She finally relented, and upon entering was introduced to a new friend: Mrs. Dick Riley, wife of South Carolina's former governor, whom the agents were protecting.

Thrasher's serves thousands of hot dogs each day, many as take-out orders. A week doesn't go by that an order of a thousand hot dogs is not placed by a local factory. The hot dogs themselves are specially made for the restaurant, as are the buns. The chili, a must even if you are not a chili fan, is a secret recipe closely guarded by the family. To make the meal complete, order a Coca-Cola in a glass bottle—something that even the sons who now run the establishment admit is getting harder and harder to find.

Adorning the walls of the old building are pictures of well-known personalities who have dined there. Actors, athletes, politicians, and even the San Diego Chicken have all had the famous hot dogs. Everyone in Anderson eats at Thrasher's at one time or another, so be careful there isn't someone present you don't want to see. One day a man walked in and ordered two dogs and a beer. Just then he looked at the other end of the counter and saw a familiar face. "Cancel that beer and give me a Coke," he said softly to the waitress. "I'm on probation, and that's Judge Frank Epps sitting over there!"

The restaurant has been featured in the *Atlanta Journal* and *Charlotte Observer* newspapers, and National Public Radio broadcast live from there following the 1994 congressional elections. While there are now five locations throughout the Upstate, you need to visit the original location to get the true flavor and spirit of Skin Thrasher's Hot Dogs. Order two dogs and a Coke. You too will understand why the place has been around for half a century.

The Towne House

Owner or manager:	Lark Karlow
Address:	125 N. Main Street, Anderson
Directions:	From I-85, take US 76 (exit 19) S toward Anderson. After you pass the Anderson Mall, US 76 becomes Main St. Continue on Main approx. 3 mi. to Earle St. Restaurant is 1 block N of Nations Bank, between Earle and Whitner Streets.
Phone number:	864-225-9791
Hours of operation:	MON–FRI 11:00AM–2:00PM; FRI 11:00AM–2:00PM, 6:00–9:00PM; SAT 6:00–9:00AM
Payment method:	checks; major credit cards
Reservations:	recommended for evening
Dress:	casual to dressy
Gratuity:	not included
Bar:	no
Alcohol:	beer and wine
Diet/light menu:	yes
Children's menu:	no
Average price for meal:	$4.95, lunch • $14.95, dinner
Discounts:	none offered
Catering:	some
House favorites:	grilled chicken salad, seafood, sandwiches
Other:	daily lunch specials

If longevity is important to you when judging restaurants, it will be hard to ignore The Towne House in Anderson.

Lark Karlow, the current owner and proprietor since 1978, isn't sure what year the original restaurant opened. She does know that her building has housed a dining establishment for a longer tenure than any other site in town, though it had an interesting history before that.

"It was originally built as a silent movie house during the '20s and was called The Egyptian," Lark explains. "At some point in the '30s the movie house closed down and a restaurant called The Elite was opened. In the '50s a Greek family bought the restaurant and decided to change its name to The Towne House."

The business has earned a loyal following over the years, and its popularity will undoubtedly grow as Anderson begins its downtown revitalization program. Though its facade isn't particularly eye-catching, the interior has the feel of an antique store. Everything in the place is from an earlier era, from the photographs adorning the walls to the lunch counter. Illumination is provided by stained glass lamps that hang from the original pressed tin ceiling. The furnishings and Oriental rugs add elegance to the comfortable, sophisticated atmosphere. You will like The Towne House before ever tasting the food.

While many restaurant owners are not concerned how nourishing their meals are, this is not the case at The Towne House. Lark believes that food should be prepared in a healthy manner. Prior to owning the restaurant, she was a dietician at the local hospital. Her background in food taught her that "frying is not good for you." Because of this, The Towne House of-

fers many baked and broiled items as well as fresh vegetables, many of which are purchased from area farmers who deliver directly to the rear door of the restaurant. Because of this attention to preparation—which Lark handles much  of herself—many of the restaurant's customers are individuals concerned with their health or weight.

The lunch crowd is largely made up of businessmen, like attorneys, who don't have much time. It rarely takes more than five minutes to be served. Daily lunch specials include a meat and two vegetables ($4.75) or a vegetable plate (four vegetables, $4.50), both of which are served with delicious fresh baked rolls. The large selection of salads (grilled chicken and spinach with walnuts, $6.50, is a favorite) and specialty sandwiches ($5.95) are also popular items.

Evening meals are served on Fridays and Saturdays only. In addition to the regular menu, six weekend specials are offered, with fresh fish and shrimp always available. The crab cakes ($18.95) and filet mignon ($14.50) are two of the biggest sellers in the evening. Reservations are recommended. Lark's nighttime patrons are so consistent, many of them maintain weekly reservations and call only if they will not be using their table that evening.

For special occasions, The Towne House has a balcony that can accommodate groups of up to twelve people. The owner occasionally caters cocktail parties.

After her many years in the business, Lark is thankful for her loyal customers. She knows that reputation is everything in the business, and she tries to make every person's visit a special one. "I always believe that if I can get a customer to come to us once, they'll come back again."

Brannon's Seafood

Owner or manager:	Gary Brannon
Address:	105 Cherokee Avenue, Gaffney
Directions:	The eastern end of scenic highway SC 11 begins in Gaffney. From I-85, take SC 11 (exit 92) 2 mi. to downtown. At the RR tracks, turn left onto Cherokee Ave. and continue 2 blocks. Restaurant stands where the road forks.
Phone number:	864-489-9590
Hours of operation:	MON–SAT 10:00AM–9:00PM
Payment method:	checks
Reservations:	not needed
Dress:	casual
Gratuity:	not included
Bar:	no
Alcohol:	not served
Diet/light menu:	salads
Children's menu:	yes
Average price for meal:	$5.00, lunch • $8.00, dinner
Discounts:	none offered
Catering:	no
House favorites:	Calabash chicken, flounder
Other:	take-out buckets available

You wouldn't expect a place with the name Brannon's Seafood to be best known for chicken. While the restaurant does sell primarily seafood, its claim to fame is its Calabash chicken. Owner Gary Brannon explained how this came to be: "My father had started a fish market and then started to serve meals. One day in the '70s he came across a small chicken processor who marinated chicken breasts. It happened that the breasts had to be trimmed to a certain size and they were selling the excess to dog food plants for almost nothing. Since he could buy these small strips so cheaply, he came up with an idea: he would fry these chicken strips and sell them at lunch, calling

them Calabash chicken, after the small town of Calabash, North Carolina. Once people found out about them, they became the most popular thing on the menu."

Gary also likes to point out that while many other restaurants now serve Calabash chicken, his dad was the first to use that name.

Brannon's has an order counter and three rooms for seating. With its simple decor and casual atmosphere, you could imagine this place having Ocean Drive for an address. Though Gaffney is closer to the mountains than the coast, Gary prides himself on the restaurant's seafood.

A wide variety of seafood is available. A typical plate, which includes fries or baked potato, hushpuppies, and coleslaw, goes for $7; $8 for the large size. Flounder, whiting, perch, red snapper, catfish, boiled shrimp, fried shrimp, deviled crab, oysters, and scallops are among the choices. If you cannot decide on just one, there are combination plates available.

Lunch specials are offered daily, with choice of chicken, shrimp, or flounder, for $5. The food is prepared fresh, and all the seafood comes from Brannon Seafood Market, located just two blocks away. If you are in the mood for a salad, there are several choices available. The seafood salad, crab salad, and shrimp salad are all popular. There is also a children's menu.

The restaurant provides waitress service on only three days: Thursday, Friday, and Saturday.

Most of Gary's customers are from the Gaffney area and the owner says about one-third of his business is handled through the take-out window. Football weekends are especially busy as Brannon's offers buckets of chicken, shrimp, and fish that come with *fixin's* and serve about four people each—perfect for tailgating.

The family business has been in operation since 1964. Gary says he has learned that if you produce and serve a good product, people will come back. Considering their thirty-three years in business, this philosophy must hold true.

♦ Two major battles of the American Revolution took place in Cherokee County: Kings Mountain (on land shared with York County) and Cowpens.

♦ The town of Gaffney, Cherokee's county seat, has a very distinguishable water tank (visible from I-85)—it's in the shape of a giant peach.

♦ The Cherokee Foothills Scenic Highway (SC 11) runs east into Cherokee County.

The Fork Restaurant

Owner or manager:	Steve Segars and Billy Allen
Address:	305 S. Buncombe Road, Greer
Directions:	From I-85, take SC 14 (exit 56) N approx. 5 mi.to US 29 in Greer. Turn left (W) onto US 29, go approx. 2 mi. to S. Buncombe Rd. (just before K-Mart). Turn left onto S. Buncombe, continue about 1/4 mile. Restaurant is on left.
Phone number:	864-877-9544
Hours of operation:	7 DAYS A WEEK 24 hours
Payment method:	checks
Reservations:	not needed
Dress:	casual
Gratuity:	not included
Bar:	no
Alcohol:	not served
Diet/light menu:	salads
Children's menu:	yes
Average price for meal:	$ 3.95, breakfast • $4.76, lunch • $4.76, dinner
Discounts:	none offered
Catering:	no
House favorites:	country steak, mac & cheese, green beans
Other:	popular for Saturday breakfast and Sunday lunch

Many restaurants have that one customer who seems to be in the place so much he should own a share in the business. For The Fork in Greer, Billy Allen was that customer. Billy still visits the restaurant every day, though not as a customer. He decided if he was going to be there so much, he might as well invest in the place.

Steve Segars was running the restaurant, which had been a neighborhood mainstay for over twenty-five years, when he met customer Billy Allen. Steve confided to Billy how he wished he knew someone with a financial background who could manage that part of his business. Billy, who already owned one company in the area, recommended himself for the job. Steve and Billy became partners.

The family-style restaurant serves everyone from mill workers to businessmen. Its specialty is the one-meat-and-three-vegetable plate for $4.76. The menu—printed by Billy's wife on their home computer—changes daily, depending on what items they can obtain fresh. They generally offer a selection of four to five meats and about twelve vegetables. The house favorites are country style steak, green beans, and macaroni and cheese. Billy describes the mac and cheese as "more like lots of cheese with a little macaroni thrown in." If you are not all that hungry, sandwiches and salads are also available.

Billy is quick to point out that all dishes are prepared fresh. "We do everything from grinding our own meat to making our own hamburger patties. All of the desserts, such as the cobbler, are homemade as well."

If you are a late-night person, The Fork is the place for you. The restaurant stays open twenty-four hours and is a popular breakfast spot.

Billy explained why the doors to the place never lock: "We were opening at 6:00 AM, which meant that someone had to start coming in at 4:00 to start cooking. It was pretty difficult to hire people for that hour. We found it easier to hire someone to work from midnight until 8:00, so Steve and I decided to be open twenty-four hours."

The restaurant's busiest time is Sunday afternoon. While the place seats well over one hundred, the church crowds all seem to descend at once. The owners know they'd better serve good food to people who have to stand in line for Sunday lunch.

Although the restaurant is surrounded by all the major chain restaurants, The Fork holds its own. "We try to give the customers something that tastes fresh and homemade," Billy says, "so that they keep coming back."

McBees Diner

Owner or manager:	Gail McBee
Address:	1005 Buncombe Street, Greenville
Directions:	From I-85, take I-185 downtown. Road becomes Church St. at about 3 miles. Go 1 mile past Bi-Lo Center (coliseum), turn left onto Academy. Cross Main; Academy merges with Buncombe after 1 mile. Follow Buncombe for about a mile. Restaurant is on left, back off the road.
Phone number:	864-235-2559
Hours of operation:	MON–FRI 7:00AM–3:00PM
Payment method:	local checks
Reservations:	not needed
Dress:	casual
Gratuity:	not included
Bar:	no
Alcohol:	not served
Diet/light menu:	no
Children's menu:	no
Average price for meal:	$5.00
Discounts:	none offered
Catering:	yes
House favorites:	fried chicken, all vegetables, sweet potato pie
Other:	take-out available

McBee's Diner in Greenville is a hidden gem. When informed that her restaurant had been chosen to be included in this book, owner Gail McBee's first reaction was, "How did you hear about this place?"

While many of Greenville's restaurants try to impress their patrons by being trendy and hip, McBee's has survived solely on the hard work of the owner and great food.

Located for years on Pendleton Street, the restaurant fell victim to arson in the summer of 1997 and was completely destroyed. Gail refused to be deterred, and soon reopened her restaurant to the delight of her loyal clientele.

The change in location has been a plus for visitors to McBee's. The original building had very little seating, and privacy was non-existent. The new building (originally Ham House Restaurant) has much more room and, therefore, more seating. The diversity of the customers has not changed. Gail serves everyone from laborers to bank presidents.

The McBees happened into the business when the owner of a local restaurant informed them he was selling out. At the time, they had no experience in the field. Gail explained how they made the decision to purchase a restaurant: "My husband came home one day and asked if I wanted to do something that would help our children. He said that by running a restaurant the family could spend more time together. I said, 'Let's do it.'"

That decision turned out to be a good one. Gail has been able to put her two daughters through college because of the diner, and now has grandchildren who help out there. She says she is already preparing for her daughters to take over when she decides to retire.

The food is a mix of soul food and country cooking. Upon entering the diner, you proceed to the food counter located at the back of the room. A meal consists of one meat and one or more vegetables. The price is dictated by the number of vegetables you choose: one, $3.65; two, $4.15; three, $4.65; four, $5.30. The hardest decision you will face is not what to get, but what not to get.

"Everything here is homemade," Gail said. "I use a lot of recipes that were passed down from my momma to my sister and myself. We try to offer something for everyone."

Beef stew, fried chicken, and baked fish are offered everyday, along with one additional meat, such as liver, pot pie, or ribs. The vegetables vary, though the sweet potato pie, macaroni and cheese, and broccoli and cheese casserole are the three favorites.

If you still have room when you've made it through your dinner plate, the peach cobbler and banana pudding are both excellent ways to end a good meal.

"We started off small," Gail explained. "At the beginning we had just one cook and myself and we did primarily short-order items. As the restaurant grew, I saw a need for a change and made it into what I have today."

When you're in the mood to enjoy good food and make new friends, McBee's Diner might be just the place for you.

♦ Baseball pitcher Nolan Ryan spent his first year of minor league play in Greenville.

♦ Greenville County was home to baseball legend "Shoeless Joe" Jackson.

Olympian

Owner or manager:	Steve Georgopoulos
Address:	743 Congaree Road, Greenville
Directions:	From I-385 (which runs from I-85 NW to Greenville), take Haywood Road exit left toward Haywood Mall. At first traffic light, turn left onto Congaree Road; continue approx. 1 mile to restaurant.
Phone number:	864-288-0300
Hours of operation:	MON–THU 11:00AM–10:00PM; FRI 11:00AM–10:30PM; SAT 9:00AM–10:30PM
Payment method:	major credit cards
Reservations:	not needed
Dress:	casual
Gratuity:	included for groups of 8 or more
Bar:	no
Alcohol:	beer and wine
Diet/light menu:	salads, pasta dishes
Children's menu:	yes
Average price for meal:	$7.50
Discounts:	none offered
Catering:	some
House favorites:	lasagna, calzones
Other:	bakery next door

Greece has always been known for two things: the Olympic games and good food. South Carolina is blessed in having a number of excellent Greek restaurants within its borders. For residents of the Upstate, there is one particularly noteworthy for its excellence in both Greek and Italian cuisine.

That place is the Olympian. It started small but has continued to expand in size and service—due to the work of its owner, Steve Georgopoulos. Over the years the Olympian has developed a loyal clientele in the Greenville area.

Unlike many of his Greek brethren, Steve did not grow up in the business. "I went to school at Mars Hill in North Carolina to play soccer. While there I got a job in a restaurant as a cook. After I had been there for awhile, I knew I wanted to have my own place."

Steve moved to Greenville in 1984 to join a relative who was living in the area. Though he later lived in Massachusetts and Atlanta, he was drawn to the South Carolina Upstate. "My wife was in school in Atlanta," he said. "I looked around that city and decided there were too many other places that were similar to what I wanted to start. When I found this location, we were about the only restaurant around."

Though the Olympian now has increased competition (almost every franchise you can name has moved into this choice vicinity) Steve's establishment has flourished. This can no doubt be attributed to the wide range of items on the menu, the reasonable prices, and the fact that everything is good. The specialty entreés are divided evenly between Greek and Italian. The owner says he can't really name one dish that is a favorite. He enjoys the chicken souvlaki ($7.95), the lasagna (with choices of mushrooms, meatballs, or sausage, $8.75), and the calzones ($5.95). Specials, such as grape leaves stuffed with ground beef and rice, are offered daily. Pizzas, subs, and specialty sandwiches (such as the gyro, $4.25) are also offered.

"Almost all my recipes are ones I got from my family," Steve explains. "Greeks really enjoy their food."

Steve spends most of his time in the Olympian's kitchen with his brother, while his sister works out front with the customers.

With the restaurant established and successful, Steve wanted to expand his operation. When the tenant in the building next door moved out, he knew it was time. He opened Olympian's International Market. Run by his parents, the market offers an assortment of breads, cheeses, and desserts.

"There were two reasons I named this place Olympian. One was to let people know that we are Greek, and the other was to express my love of athletics."

Though you won't get any gold medals at the Olympian, Steve promises you will get a winning meal.

The Open Hearth

Owner or manager:	Jimmy Melehes
Address:	2801 Wade Hampton Blvd., Greenville
Directions:	From intersection of US 29 (Wade Hampton Blvd.) and SC 291 (Pleasantburg Rd.), follow US 29 NE (toward Spartanburg) approx. 3 miles. Restaurant is on left, in Hampton Village Shopping Center.
Phone number:	864-232-6727
Hours of operation:	MON–SAT 5:30–10:00PM
Payment method:	major credit cards
Reservations:	recommended
Dress:	casual to dressy
Gratuity:	not included
Bar:	yes
Alcohol:	yes
Diet/light menu:	salads, fish
Children's menu:	no
Average price for meal:	$12.95
Discounts:	none offered
Catering:	in-house only—private rooms available for groups of 8 to 20
House favorites:	all cuts of steak
Other:	good wine selection

People familiar with dining in Chicago know that the Windy City is famous for its steakhouses. Unlike the franchise steakhouses to which most of us in the South are accustomed, the steakhouses of Chicago are upscale, sophisticated restaurants that cook their food on an open grill.

Residents of Greenville are fortunate to have such a restaurant in their own community. The Open Hearth, owned and operated by Jimmy Melehes, has been in business since 1959. And it is no accident that his restaurant resembles the famous steakhouses of Illinois's largest city.

"My father, Mike, was in the restaurant business downtown" (his cousin was the owner of Greenville's well-known Pete's Restaurant) "working eighteen hours a day," explains Jimmy. "His family had immigrated to Chicago from Greece when he was young and he knew all about the famous steakhouses. He decided to open up his own place so he went to Chicago to study the steakhouses there. He came back and opened his place in that style."

Among the advantages to owning his own restaurant was the freedom to set his work hours. Mike wanted to open just in the evening. "He wanted to be able to spend more time at home," Jimmy said, "though he soon discovered golf and was gone on the course everyday."

In naming his new restaurant, Mike decided to use a name that would tell how his meals are prepared. As the trademark of the place was to be its large open grill, the name Open Hearth seemed appropriate.

Jimmy cites the restaurant's cooking method as one of the keys to Open Hearth's success. "Our grill uses real charcoal bricks, not gas," he says. "We use fresh charcoal each day. This allows the flavor to be seered in without drying out the meat."

As you can imagine, the restaurant is best known for its steaks. There is a large selection of cuts from which to choose: sirloin, New York strip, T-bone, filet mignon, ribeye, and shish kebab. Prices range from $12.59 to $17.95 and include potato, onion rings, and a salad. When asked to name which steak is the best, Jimmy says it is just personal choice.

"People ask us all the time what they should get, and I always tell them I don't know. It depends on what kind of cut you like the best. No matter what you get, you shouldn't be disappointed."

Those who are not big on red meat shouldn't be dissuaded from trying this place. Jimmy says he believes his pork chops, chicken, and fish are on par with his steaks. Seafood lovers have a variety of options, including salmon ($14.95), grouper ($15.95), swordfish steak ($16.95), lobster tails ($29.95), and rainbow trout ($11.95).

Jimmy says people enjoy his restaurant because it has the family touch. His father died several years ago, but there is always at least one member of the Melehes family greeting customers at the door. And, most of the staff has been at the restaurant for many years. The current cook has worked the grill for ten years, following in the footsteps of another who retired after forty-five years of employment with the family.

Jimmy began working at The Open Hearth as a teenager, before going away to college in Columbia. He was planning to get a law degree but got tired of school. "Looking back," he says, "it's the best decision I ever made."

♦ The Peace Center for the Performing Arts is one of the more eye-catching pieces of architecture in downtown Greenville.

♦ South Carolina's only standing covered bridge can be found in Greenville County.

Harry's Old-Fashioned Hamburgers

Owner or manager:	Jo and Greg Mull
Address:	200 E. Willard Street, Clinton
Directions:	From I-26, take SC 56 (exit 52) S (Willard St.) 2-1/2 mi. to downtown Clinton. Restaurant is on left, across from Bi-Lo.
Phone number:	864-938-1096
Hours of operation:	MON–SAT 24 hours
Payment method:	checks
Reservations:	not needed
Dress:	casual
Gratuity:	not included
Bar:	no
Alcohol:	not served
Diet/light menu:	no
Children's menu:	no
Average price for meal:	$3.00, breakfast • $4.00, lunch • $4.00, dinner
Discounts:	none offered
Catering:	no
House favorites:	hot dogs, bird dogs, wings
Other:	popular, no matter what time of day or night

When people in Clinton get a craving for a big, juicy hamburger, they don't think about McDonald's or Burger King. They know the place to go is Harry's Old-Fashioned Hamburgers, run by Greg and Jo Hull.

The restaurant was originally opened by Harry Agnew, a former state legislator. Agnew sold a percentage of the business to the Hulls who manage the twenty-four-hour restaurant.

Jo says she loves her restaurant despite all the work. "Even though I put in eighteen-hour days, I love every minute of it. I am a people person and the people who come in here have become my friends and family. There are probably about 500 people I consider regulars. It's not the whole town yet, but we're working on it."

The restaurant serves a number of different sandwiches, salads, hot dogs, and shrimp. But the hamburgers are by far the most popular items. You can choose the regular hamburger ($3.39), the cheeseburger ($3.49), the bacon cheeseburger ($3.99), or the double cheeseburger ($4.99).

Jo says she uses over 600 pounds of hamburger meat a week. Besides the burgers, the bird dog (chicken strips on a hot dog bun) and chicken wings are the other big sellers. "I serve 400 pounds of chicken fingers and 600 pounds of wings every week. My food distributor just loves me," Jo declares.

Closed on Sundays, the doors of Harry's remain open around the clock throughout the week. Jo says she serves about 700 people a day, with many eating two and three of their daily meals there. Some of her patrons are so punctual she can set her watch by them. And unlike many places that stay open all night, she never worries about getting robbed, thanks in part to her popularity with law enforcement.

"We serve almost every police officer in this area: city police, county deputies, highway patrol, SLED. There aren't too many times when there isn't some kind of officer in here," she says.

Being close to Presbyterian College isn't bad for business either. The restaurant is a big supporter of the school and its athletic programs. Jo feeds the baseball team at least once during the season. "Those boys can really eat," she says.

With only six booths and four tables, the place can fill up in a hurry. With its popularity, one might think the Hulls would want to expand their small place to accommodate more customers. But Jo says they wouldn't think of it.

"We're not in this to make a million dollars. Our goal is to make our customers happy. That's why I come to work. I'm not going to try to fix something that's not broken."

Steak House Cafeteria

Owner or manager:	Abed and Gloria Israel
Address:	316 E. Main Street, Walhalla
Directions:	SC 28 forms Main St. in the tiny town of Walhalla (about 8 mi. NW of Seneca and 20 mi. N of I-85). The restaurant is easy to find, nestled among the few buildings that make up downtown.
Phone number:	864-638-3311
Hours of operation:	TUE-WED 11:00AM–2:30PM, THU-SAT 11:00AM–8:00PM, SUN 11:00AM–2:30PM
Payment method:	local checks
Reservations:	not accepted
Dress:	casual
Gratuity:	not included
Bar:	no
Alcohol:	not served
Diet/light menu:	vegetables
Children's menu:	no
Average price for meal:	$6.00
Discounts:	none offered
Catering:	no
House favorites:	fried chicken

Ask just about anyone in Oconee County, "the Golden Triangle of South Carolina," what the locals' favorite restaurant is, and the answer is almost universally "Steak House Cafeteria."

When you decide to go to the cafeteria, expect good food—just don't expect any steaks. Many first-time visitors wonder how a place can get away with calling itself The Steak House when it doesn't even offer what its name advertises. The truth lies in the fact that the restaurant has been around for about sixty years and until the 1970s it did serve steaks. All this changed when Abed Israel took over its operation.

Abed, originally from Palestine, married Gloria Cleveland, a local girl, and settled in the area. When he took over the restaurant, he changed its focus.

"I decided that people in the South love fried chicken, so I wanted to specialize in that," says the friendly Abed. "The problem was that in Israel they don't fry chicken, so I needed a recipe." He began experimenting with frying techniques.

He decided, instead of regular fryer parts, to use red rooster breasts. These huge, juicy breasts have become the trademark of the restaurant. Most people don't believe that only one chicken breast will fill them up, but at The Steak House Cafeteria it will. Abed now serves between 2100 and 2500 pounds of chicken each week. *Blue Ridge Magazine* called it the best fried chicken in the Blue Ridge Mountains. Though the place could now accurately be called Chicken House Cafeteria, Abed wouldn't think of disturbing the restaurant's legacy by changing its name.

The food is served cafeteria style, and you are charged for each item you order. In addition to chicken, a variety of other

meats, such as ham and turkey, is offered. There are always a half-dozen or so vegetables from which to select. (If they have carrots, get them. You wouldn't believe carrots could be this good!) If your eyes are bigger than your stomach, you may choose to add a fruit salad or dessert, such as coconut pie or chocolate cake, to your plate. The price for an average meal ranges from $5 to $7.

Besides the food, there is another reason the place is so popular: Abed. The locals pronounce his name "Abby," but he doesn't mind what you call him. He oversees all the preparation of the food, and will prepare specialty items for good customers that call ahead. Once the restaurant fills up, Abed spends much of his time visiting with patrons to gossip about local news. His outgoing disposition and white apron make it easy to recognize him.

Abed has two dining rooms and a third under construction, but he admits surprise at being successful. "I have exceeded my expectations. But I have always believed that if you are willing to work hard, good things will happen to you."

♦ The picturesque town of Walhalla, Oconee's county seat, was settled by German immigrants. Residents celebrate their heritage each year with an Oktoberfest.

Sardi's Den

Owner or manager:	Mike McHenry and Irv Harrington
Address:	520 #2 SC 93, Clemson
Directions:	From the intersection of US 76/123 and SC 93 in Clemson, follow SC 93 NE (toward Greenville) approx. 2 miles. Restaurant is on right, in front of Bi-Lo.
Phone number:	864-654-RIBS
Hours of operation:	MON–SAT 11:30AM–11:00PM
Payment method:	checks
Reservations:	recommended Tuesday evening
Dress:	casual
Gratuity:	not included
Bar:	yes
Alcohol:	yes
Diet/light menu:	grilled chicken, salads, shrimp
Children's menu:	no
Average price for meal:	$8.00
Discounts:	none offered
Catering:	yes
House favorites:	ribs, ribeye, chicken wings
Other:	take-out party platters available

When Mike McHenry and Irv Harrington met on the football field in 1985, it's doubtful they ever thought they would end up as business partners. But their friendship, which started on the gridiron, has extended into the restaurant world. The two now own and run Sardi's Den in Clemson.

Mike and Irv were college students when they became friends. "We met while playing club football at Clemson," Mike said. "Both of us had to work to help pay our way through school, so we got jobs at the Lazy Islander Restaurant in Pendleton. We started out as waiters but eventually moved up to where Irv was the [general] manager and I was the kitchen manager."

After graduating, Irv getting his degree in building science and Mike in industrial engineering, the two went to work for a business in Clemson. After a couple of years, they realized they would never get ahead by working for someone else, so they decided to go into business for themselves.

At that same time the opportunity to buy Sardi's presented itself. "Irv's family knew who started the restaurant and found out they were looking to sell it. Irv and I decided that there wouldn't be any better time to make our best shot," Mike explains.

The restaurant is best known for its baby back ribs, its signature dish, served as a half rack ($5.85), full rack ($9.95), or big rack ($13.50). Tiger fans routinely stop in on game day and pick up a take-out order to add to their tailgate. After taking over the restaurant, Mike said he and his partner knew they would keep the ribs but wanted to make some alterations in the menu.

"We probably changed about half the menu to suit what our specialties were when we came in. Irv and I have evolved as the menu has. At first I handled the kitchen while he handled the outside management. However, I showed him how to do everything in the kitchen while he showed me how the management stuff works. This really enables us to be effective."

Besides ribs, Sardi's also sells pound after pound of chicken wings. And, if you like blackened dishes, you are in luck. Chicken, shrimp, and ribeye are served—very spicy or lightly spiced.

There are popular daily specials too: Monday is Italian, Tuesday is all-you-can-eat crab legs, Wednesday is one-dollar-off ribs, and Thursday is seafood. Mike recommends you make a reservation for the crab leg feast on Tuesday.

Though located on the outskirts of town, Mike says about twenty-five percent of their customers are students or people connected with the university.

Their success has allowed them to expand to a second location in nearby Anderson. "We thought that since we were doing so well," Mike said, "we should try our luck with a second restaurant."

Those of us who have enjoyed the tasty meals at Sardi's Den know that luck has nothing to do with the restaurant's popularity. As long as Mike and Irv keep up the good cooking, the customers will keep coming.

♦ John Heisman (of Heisman Trophy fame) once coached football at Clemson University. He is said to have chosen the Tiger as the school's mascot, as well as the school colors of orange and purple.

♦ Pickens County is home to two state parks.

Villa Luigi

Owner or manager:	Louis Sardinas
Address:	217 W. Main Street, Central
Directions:	SC 93 forms Main St. in the small town of Central (about 5 miles NE of Clemson). The restaurant is prominent among the buildings that make up the short stretch of Main downtown. Entering town from Clemson, the restaurant is on the right.
Phone number:	864-639-0076
Hours of operation:	MON–SAT 4:30–10:00PM*
Payment method:	checks, major credit cards
Reservations:	recommended on weekend
Dress:	casual to dressy
Gratuity:	not included
Bar:	yes
Alcohol:	yes
Diet/light menu:	lighter items available
Children's menu:	no
Average price for meal:	$6.95, lunch • $9.95, dinner
Discounts:	none offered
Catering:	weddings, private parties
House favorites:	lasagna, seafood, steaks
Other:	patio dining (weather permitting) *call for lunch hours during FALL

In a town the size of Central, you might expect the only place to eat is an old filling station selling nothing but stale sandwiches and boiled peanuts. Little would you expect to come across a place like Villa Luigi, an Italian restaurant that combines wonderful cuisine and charm.

People questioned owner Louis Sardinas's decision to open such a place in a town so small. But while others were skeptical, Louis saw a diamond in the rough.

"The town of Clemson has been booming the last few years, and the growth is in this direction, toward Central. We are only four miles from the heart of the university, so I see this area expanding as well. And, right now, this is the only place of its kind around," Louis explained.

He should know what he's talking about, having worked in the restaurant business for close to twenty years. Louis, who immigrated from Cuba when Castro went into power, originally managed restaurants in Florida before moving to the South Carolina Upstate ten years ago. Since arriving, he has owned a gourmet restaurant in downtown Greenville and established Sardi's Den in Clemson. He said he now has the type of place he always wanted—not too large or small, but a size where he can try many different things.

As the name would suggest, the restaurant specializes in entrees from throughout Italy. While he could not pick one particular favorite, Louis says the lasagna ($7.78), smoked chicken ravioli ($8.97), and pork piccata (boneless pork tenderloin sauteed in olive oil, with capers, wild mushrooms, and artichokes, $10.85) are excellent. He offers two or three nightly specials (usually seafood) and is constantly adding new items to the menu. He is planning to install a lobster tank, which will allow customers to choose their own live Maine lobsters.

If you have a picky eater in the crowd, don't worry. "We prepare everything to order," Louis said. "Even if you want something that is not on the menu, just ask. If we have the ingredients in the kitchen, we'll prepare it for you."

The building that houses Villa Luigi is one of the primary reasons Louis chose Central as the location for his restaurant. It dates to the Civil War and is on the town's list of historic sites. Congressman Lindsey Graham grew up in the house. Graham's family sold the property to Louis. The building was in disrepair at the time Louis purchased it, and he spent eight months getting it in shape to serve as a restaurant. Though much of the structure had to be replaced, he took great pains to keep as much of the original as possible.

If the weather is favorable, many guests like to eat outside on the patio located in the front courtyard. Louis envisioned

this area as simply a place where his patrons would have cocktails before heading inside to dine, but he has been surprised at its popularity. "Some nights every seat outside is taken and others are waiting for tables even if there is plenty of room available inside."

The restaurant's walls are filled with signs and photographs depicting Italy and Italian tenements in New York City. If they look familiar to you, there is a reason for that. "When the Tomato Rumba chain went bankrupt," Louis explained, "I went to several auctions and bought all of their decorations. I had always liked them, and they are perfect for an Italian place," Louis explained.

The core of Villa Luigi's clientelle is made up of people connected with Clemson University: students, professors, and alumni. Fall is the beginning of the busy season at the restaurant, and the owner recommends calling for reservations on weekends.

Mimi's

Owner or manager:	Tim Holmes
Address:	180 E. Main Street, Spartanburg
Directions:	US 29 (which crosses both I-85 and I-26 just W of Spartanburg) forms Main Street. Restaurant is downtown on Main, across from BB&T tower.
Phone number:	864-585-8332
Hours of operation:	MON–FRI 11:00AM–3:30PM
Payment method:	checks
Reservations:	not needed
Dress:	casual
Gratuity:	not included
Bar:	no
Alcohol:	not served
Diet/light menu:	salads, sandwiches
Children's menu:	no
Average price for meal:	$5.00
Discounts:	none offered
Catering:	yes
House favorites:	chicken salad, reuben, turkey breast sandwich

Before Tim Holmes opened Mimi's deli in Spartanburg, he was working very long hours in the grocery business. His father recognized all his hard work and gave him some advice. "Dad told me if I was going to work this hard, I might as well be working for myself," Tim says. "I thought about this and decided he was right."

Tim grew up in Mexico where his parents had gone as missionaries. When the family moved back to the states, they located in Greenville, where Tim graduated from Bob Jones University.

Tim decided to open a restaurant. He had some experience in the restaurant business, having served as a manager for Wendy's. The problem Tim faced in opening his own place was

deciding what kind of restaurant to start. He saw that there was not an upscale deli in Spartanburg and felt the market could use one. Now, eight successful years later, it is obvious he made a good choice.

Mimi's is located in the heart of downtown Spartanburg directly across from the BB&T tower in a building that formerly served as a hot dog eatery. Tim redecorated the interior with bright, fresh colors and added small tables with tableclothes. It wasn't long before the new decor attracted bankers, doctors, and lawyers.

"A friend of mine was in one day and recognized that many of the customers were attorneys," Tim said. "He told me that if anyone ever wanted to get rid of all the lawyers in town, all they would have to do is set a bomb in my restaurant."

The deli serves cafeteria style, so you can watch your order put together right in front of you. The most popular item is the chicken salad (sandwich, $4.59; salad plate, $4.99). The turkey club and the reuben ($4.59 each) are also big sellers. If you're feeling a little more creative, you can combine two meats (roast beef, turkey breast, ham, salami, pepperoni, pastrami), and one kind of cheese on your choice of bread (white, wheat, pumpernickel, rye, or sub roll) to create the perfect sandwich (regular, $4.59; large, $5.79). Several salads, all made fresh daily, are available.

If you're in the mood for dessert at the end of your meal, Mimi's offers more than a dozen flavors of ice cream. They also have terrific homemade cookies.

Tim now owns two other restaurants—a bagel shop and a tea room—and he runs a catering business, handling dinners of up to 1,500 people. His wife is involved heavily in the business and, according to Tim, helps him keep everything straight.

♦ South Carolina's official state folk dance is the square dance.

Woodward's Cafe

Owner or manager:	Charles Whitmire
Address:	438 Stevens St., Spartanburg
Directions:	From I-26, take US 29 (exit 21) E toward downtown, about 4 mi. to US 221. Cross US 221 and continue approx. 1/2 mi. to Thompson St. Turn left onto Thompson and go 2 blocks to Stevens St. Restaurant is at corner of Stevens and Thompson.
Phone number:	864-585-5986
Hours of operation:	MON–FRI 11:00AM–1:30PM
Payment method:	cash only
Reservations:	not needed
Dress:	casual
Gratuity:	not included
Bar:	no
Alcohol:	not served
Diet/light menu:	no
Children's menu:	yes
Average price for meal:	$5.50
Discounts:	none offered
Catering:	no
House favorites:	fried chicken, sweet potato pie

When Robert Woodward decided to open a small café in this Spartanburg neighborhood, he planned to keep his prices reasonable. After looking at what his costs would be and what residents in the neighborhood could affor,d he decided to charge ten cents a plate. If, after the meal, you were in the mood for a smoke, he would sell you half a cigarette for a penny. This was in 1928, when Woodward's Cafe first opened its doors.

The original owner has since passed, but the establishment is still going strong under the management of Charles Whitmire, Woodward's nephew. "Uncle Robert had been running the place for about thirty years and decided it was time to retire," Charles explains. "I was working for him at the time and he allowed me to take over."

If ever there was a restaurant off the beaten track, Woodward's Cafe is it. Nestled in an old mill neighborhood, the building is nothing more than a shotgun house that Woodward converted. If there wasn't a metal sign outside, you would never guess it was a restaurant. After walking through a screened-in porch, you enter a small dining room with six tables and a counter. An old floor furnace heats the dining room and kitchen. The interior appears to have been kept in its original condition, from the pine wood floor to the beadboard walls.

"We have never thought about moving anywhere," Charles explains. "This place survives on word of mouth alone." The out-of-the-way restaurant has, in fact, been featured on television and in newspapers several times over the years.

An African-American, Woodward opened his place to serve the black community of Spartanburg. In time, word spread through town and whites began showing up with or-

ders. That was a problem during the time of segregation. Whites and blacks did not dine together—and certainly would not have shared tables.

Woodward found a way to solve the problem and increase his business. He went outside to take orders from white customers and then carried their food out to them. They would eat in their cars or take the food home. Old Spartanburg residents say that many people back then would come home with food and lie about where they got it—though everyone knew it had come from Woodward's.

The menu is fairly basic. A meal costs about $6 and includes a meat (chicken, pork chops, or beef stew) and three vegetables. Vegetable choices include cabbage, rice, green beans, mashed potatoes, black-eyed peas, and lima beans. A slice of egg custard or sweet potato pie ($1.60 each) is a good way to end a meal.

♦ In 1996, video poker machines reportedly netted over $2 billion in gross revenue in South Carolina—more than Georgia grossed on its state lottery.

Heart Family Restaurant

Owner or manager:	Chris Bardis
Address:	US 176, Union
Directions:	From Spartanburg, follow US 176 S to Union city limits. Continue for several miles. Restaurant is on right, just past Quincy's.
Phone number:	864-427-7000
Hours of operation:	MON–SAT 11:00AM–9:00PM
Payment method:	checks
Reservations:	not accepted
Dress:	casual
Gratuity:	not included
Bar:	no
Alcohol:	not served
Diet/light menu:	salad bar
Children's menu:	no
Average price for meal:	$5.00
Discounts:	none offered
Catering:	no
House favorites:	hamburger steak plate

In recent years, savvy entrepreneurs reintroduced Americans to the drive-in restaurant. Across the country a variety of places catering to customers who prefer dining in their cars have cropped up. Although this idea may be new and exciting to many people, residents of Union have been dining this way for over thirty-five years at Heart Family Restaurant.

Gus Diamadurus arrived in the United States from Greece in the '50s. Although his family were farmers in his native country, his father decided to open a restaurant in Chester soon after moving here. Gus followed suit a few years later in Union.

Drive-in restaurants were all the rage in the early '60s, so Gus decided that was the sort of place he wanted. He remembers clearly his first week in business. "We opened on a Monday," he said. "President Kennedy was shot that Friday."

In the early days, ten outdoor drive-ups served the majority of Gus's customers, under a tin canopy sporting the words "Eat at Night by Moon Light." Inside, a long dining bar with nineteen stools accommodated those few who preferred to dine indoors.

The popularity of drive-ins waned over the next decade, but Gus remained in continuous operation, keeping his carhops busy. He eventually expanded the interior, replacing the dining bar with tables and chairs.

In the mid-1990s, Gus retired, selling the restaurant to Chris Bardis, the current owner. But don't be surprised to hear a Greek accent from the older gentleman working the register. "My wife and I don't need too much 'happy time' together, so I come up here," Gus explains.

The house special at Heart Family Restaurant is the hamburger steak plate. While other restaurants may disagree that it is "the world's best hamburger steak," as the menu proclaims, it certainly has to be one of the world's biggest. Covering the full length of a serving plate, it's like three hamburger steaks rolled into one. Served with coleslaw (which the menu claims is the best in town), French fries, and two slices of Texas toast, the meal is a steal at only $4.00.

Not quite that hungry? You'll have no problem finding other items to your liking. Sandwiches include barbecue ($2.25), BLT ($2.10), and jumbo cheeseburger ($3.50). Seafood selections include shrimp ($7.95) and flounder ($5.75). There is also a salad bar ($3.50). If you have room for dessert, there is a variety of pies to choose from.

Today, Heart Family Restaurant doesn't do nearly the carhop business it did during the '60s, but it stays just as busy. And you have a choice of eating inside at a table or having a carhop deliver right to your car.

Heart Family Restaurant is a place the whole family will enjoy.

The Coal Yard Restaurant

Owner or manager:	Joe Forlines
Address:	105 Garner Street, York
Directions:	From the intersection of US 321 BYPASS and SC 5 (Liberty St.) in town, follow SC 5 E about 5 blocks to Garner Street. Turn left on Garner. Restaurant is only business at that point.
Phone number:	864-684-9653
Hours of operation:	MON–FRI 11:00AM–MIDNIGHT SAT 5:00PM–MIDNIGHT
Payment method:	checks
Reservations:	not accepted
Dress:	casual
Gratuity:	not included
Bar:	yes
Alcohol:	yes
Diet/light menu:	salads, chicken
Children's menu:	no
Average price for meal:	steaks, $12.95 • sandwiches, $4.95
Discounts:	none offered
Catering:	no
House favorites:	steaks, stuffed potatoes
Other:	bar area to rear of restaurant

Many restaurant owners boast that they went into the business to satisfy a lifelong goal. But for Joe Forlines, the owner of The Coal Yard Restaurant in York, opening a restaurant had never crossed his mind before he did it.

"I had often thought it might be fun to own a bar," Joe said, "and I hoped at some point I would have the chance to open one. I had known people in the restaurant business and I wasn't really interested in doing it myself."

Life has taken a series of unexpected turns for Joe. Born in Missouri and raised in California, he was surprised one day when the company he worked for decided to transfer him to faraway South Carolina. Soon after the move, Joe became dissatisfied with his new position and decided it might be the right time to open his bar. He asked friends about his idea and was surprised what he heard.

"Everyone I mentioned my bar idea to," Joe reports, "said they thought it was fine, but believed what York really needed was a restaurant where you could get a drink. At that time you either had to drive to Charlotte or Rock Hill if you wanted someplace to take your wife or girlfriend that served both food and alcohol. The more I thought about it, the more it became apparent that a restaurant is what I should open."

He found an old grocery store near downtown that until the end of the 1960s had been used to sell coal to people. Since the locals in town referred to the building as the coal yard, Joe decided to adopt it as the name of his new place. He opened the restaurant in 1979 and has been going strong ever since.

Walking into the establishment, the first thing you notice is that the walls are covered with posters and memorabilia. Explaining his decorating scheme, Joe points out that the train once ran right by the place, so he started out with a railroad motif. Soon, he said, he began picking up odds and ends from different places and hanging them. He finally used up all wall space, so he rarely buys anything new these days.

The top attraction on the menu is steak. Joe said he is known for serving large steaks at reasonable prices. Most people, he declares, can't finish his ribeye, a sixteen-ounce cut of western beef served with potato, bread, and a trip to the salad bar ($13.95.) Most regulars have learned—unless they are close to starvation—to get the Coal Yard Cut (a smaller portion at $12.95).

Another favorite is Joe's stuffed baked potatoes, known as Coal Yard Taters. Patrons have four choices: the greater tater (stuffed with ham, turkey, roast beef, peppers, onion, and mushrooms, topped with cheese, $3.95), the chicken salad tater (stuffed with chicken salad and shredded cheddar and provolone cheeses, $3.95), the vegetarian tater (stuffed with cheese, peppers, and onions, $3.25), or a plain old tater. The menu includes a variety of items: chicken strips, calabash shrimp, sandwiches, and salad bar.

The bar area is at the rear of the restaurant where people once picked up their coal.

"I always say this place is like *Cheers*—everyone knows everyone here," Joe remarks. "Many people come in early to eat and then spend the rest of the evening in the lounge. Others finish their meals and remain at their tables to talk the night away. I don't ask anyone to give up a table, even if I have a line of people waiting."

After seventeen years in the business, Joe admits his place is still a secret even among residents of York. He often runs into people who have never heard of The Coal Yard Restaurant. With only one small sign on the side of the building, it is easy to miss. But once they discover the place, they invariably make their way back.

♦ The Catawba Indian Reservation, the only Indian reservation in South Carolina, is located in York County on the Catawba River.

♦ Some may remember York County as the home of Jim and Tammy Faye Baker and Heritage USA.

Ebenezer Grill

Owner or manager:	Doug Herlong
Address:	1525 Ebenezer Rd., Rock Hill
Directions:	From I-77, take SC 161 (exit 82) W about 4-1/2 miles to SC 274 (Ebenezer Rd.). Turn left and follow SC 274 SE approx. 2mi. Restaurant is on left, about 1 block past Founders Federal bank.
Phone number:	803-327-6700
Hours of operation:	MON–FRI 6:00AM–6:00PM*, SAT 7:00AM–3:00PM
Payment method:	checks
Reservations:	not needed
Dress:	casual
Gratuity:	not included
Bar:	no
Alcohol:	*Happy Hour 6:00–7:00PM
Diet/light menu:	salads, soup
Children's menu:	no
Average price for meal:	$4.00
Discounts:	none
Catering:	no
House favorites:	hot dogs, homemade soup
Other:	delivery available in immediate area, popular after-hours watering hole

Most business owners like to toot their own horns when describing the success of their enterprise. But you won't hear Doug Herlong declaring himself a genius when talking about the popularity of Ebenezer Grill.

"I don't really understand why the place is so successful," says the outgoing proprietor, "because it is really a dump. There's nothing to it. It's just a little block building with a grill. But for some reason people around here love it."

True, there is nothing in its appearance (which Doug describes as "fashionably shabby") that makes Ebenezer Grill stand out, but people keep coming back.

"The few tables I've got in here aren't nearly enough when this place gets busy during lunchtime. But I'm afraid it would lose its charm if I ever tried to change anything, so I won't."

Doug's personality is a major draw for customers. The high-spirited, fast talking owner is the type of person who becomes a good friend in about five minutes.

He had never been in the food business prior to taking over the Ebenezer Grill in 1993. When he lost his job at an area country club, he found some local investors to help him buy the restaurant. "I never thought getting fired would be the best thing to ever happen to me," he said.

While the small restaurant, which had been around for some time, was a popular spot prior to Doug's ownership, its popularity has skyrocketed since. "Business has increased 600 percent since I first came in. Word of mouth is an unbelievable thing. I have yet to do any advertising and still I have almost more customers than I can handle." Ebenezer Grill has become so busy, in fact, the flow of traffic in the area during certain hours has been affected. City officials informed Doug he would have to put signs up in front directing customers to park in back.

While the menu carries the standard fare of most small grills (hamburgers, club sandwiches, grilled cheese sandwiches), there are two items for which Ebenezer Grill is especially known: hot dogs and soup. The hot dogs, served with chili and slaw, are the best in Rock Hill. The homemade soup is the meal of choice during cold weather, when the staff prepares over 120 gallons a week. For only $3.50 (which includes a grilled cheese sandwich), you can have as much of the tasty hot dish as you want.

Doug understands how to keep his customers happy. His lunch crowd is largely made up of secretaries from the many doctors' and lawyers' offices in the area. He has two television sets in opposite corners tuned in to soap operas. Doug says you don't dare try to change the channel during that time of the day—for fear of being attacked.

The grill begins serving breakfast at 6:00 AM and serves from the lunch menu until 6:00 PM. At that hour the place becomes an informal watering hole for locals who choose to wind down from the workday with a couple beers. "I can tell what time it is during the day by what faces I see in here. After 6:00 you better be pretty thick skinned because the crowd in here can really rag you."

When visiting Ebenezer Grill, there are three things you should not miss: a hot dog, a cup of soup, and a talk with Doug Herlong.

Midlands

CALHOUN COUNTY
  Town & Country Restaurant (St. Matthews)
CHESTER COUNTY
  Catawba Fish Camp (Fort Lawn)
CLARENDON COUNTY
  Summerton Diner (Summerton)
FAIRFIELD COUNTY
  Hoot's (Winnsboro)
KERSHAW COUNTY
  Hard Times Cafe (Cassatt)
  Lucy's (Camden)
  The Paddock (Camden)
LEXINGTON COUNTY
  Cogburn's (West Columbia)
  Flight Deck (Lexington)
  Sub Cabin (West Columbia)
NEWBERRY COUNTY
  Perry's Back Porch (Prosperity)
  Ruff Brothers (Newberry)
ORANGEBURG COUNTY
  Chef's Choice Steakhouse (Eutawville)
  Chestnut Grill (Orangeburg)
RICHLAND COUNTY
  Andy's Deli (Columbia)
  Blue Marlin Seafood Kitchen (Columbia)
  Devine Foods (Columbia)
  Rockaways Athletic Club (Columbia)
SALUDA COUNTY
  Country Kitchen (Saluda)

Town & Country Restaurant

Owner or manager:	Mohamed Hloubi
Address:	103 West Bridge Street, St. Matthews
Directions:	Located downtown at corner of West Bridge Street (SC 6) and Huff Dr., at one of the town's two traffic lights—across RR tracks from US 601.
Phone number:	803-874-3900
Hours of operation:	MON–SAT 7:00AM–10:00PM, SUN 11:00AM–3:00PM
Payment method:	checks, major credit cards
Reservations:	recommended for large groups
Dress:	casual
Gratuity:	not included
Bar:	no
Alcohol:	beer and wine
Diet/light menu:	no
Children's menu:	yes
Average price for meal:	$5.00, lunch • $9.00, dinner
Discounts:	none offered
Catering:	no
House favorites:	lunch buffet
Other:	vegie dishes offered

The next time you start complaining because you have to put in a few extra hours at your job, take a second to think about Mohamed Hloubi. Mohamed, who is owner of Town & Country in St. Matthews, often works up to seventeen hours in a single day.

"I would consider a twelve-hour day to be a short day," the owner says.

Even with the long hours, Mohamed would never complain, though he admits it is sometimes difficult for his family. He often has his three children come to the restaurant just so he can see them. But he has been in the restaurant business all his working life and understands the demands of the job. In fact, he would have trouble adjusting to a typical nine-to-five workday.

"For a while I worked for my brother in a restaurant. I also have worked at a number of other restaurants." But Mohamed knew he would not get ahead by working for others. He would have to own his own place. His first venture was a place in Orangeburg, which he ran successfully. Then he heard about an intriguing opportunity in nearby St. Matthews.

The town owned a building, situated at one of its two traffic lights, that dated to the 1870s. It had been vacant for some time and the town was looking to lease the place to someone at a terrific price. The old building had the character and charm Mohamed was looking for and, although extensive renovations were needed before a restaurant could be opened, Mohamed jumped at the chance. The needed work was completed and the Town & Country was born.

The restaurant is open seven days a week, serving breakfast through dinner Monday through Saturday and lunch on Sunday. Mohamed does the majority of the cooking himself.

One of the most popular features of the restaurant is the Sunday buffet, offering a variety of meats and vegetables. At only $5.75, it is no surprise the crowds start forming soon after the final hymn is sung.

A lunch buffet is also offered during the week. For those not so hungry, there are salads and sandwiches, such as the Bubba Burger ($2.99) and the chicken fillet ($4.29). Another big seller is the submarine sandwich ($3.59 to $4.09). The price is based on how many meats you want on it (turkey, ham, salami, tuna, roast beef, bacon, and meat ball are your choices).

Mohamed offers a number of different meals in the evening, including several Italian dishes. The owner especially prides himself on the beef tips over rice ($5.99).

The next time you've put in a long day at the office, head down to Town & Country. There, you can enjoy the fruits of Mohamed's hard labor.

Catawba Fish Camp

Owner or manager:	Robert Edwards
Address:	Route 1, Fort Lawn
Directions:	From intersection of US 21 and SC 9 in tiny town of Fort Lawn (about 8 miles W of Lancaster), head E on SC 9; go about 1-1/2 miles. Restaurant on left just before Catawba River.
Phone number:	803-872-4477
Hours of operation:	WED–THU 4:00–9:30PM
	FRI-SAT 11:00AM–10:00PM
Payment method:	checks, major credit cards
Reservations:	accepted for large groups only
Dress:	casual
Gratuity:	not included
Bar:	no
Alcohol:	not served
Diet/light menu:	no
Children's menu:	yes
Average price for meal:	$8.00
Discounts:	10% to seniors
Catering:	in-house*
House favorites:	all seafood items
Other:	*available on Tuesday nights for private, reserved functions

When you walk into Catawba Fish Camp, you might feel you've entered an Army mess hall. The place is packed with row after row of tables. Your first thought is that owner Robert Edwards is crazy to think he could ever fill the place up.

But if you go back on a Friday or Saturday night and see the line of people stretching out the door, you realize what Robert really needs is *more* seating, not less. This has been true since the fish camp opened more than forty-five years ago.

Manager Phil Glover summarized the restaurant's success: "Everyone in this area knows this is a family atmosphere where they can get good food. After being in business for so long, our customers know what to expect. Some people tell us they will go to the beach for a week and come here on the day they get back just so that they can get good seafood."

The original Catawba Fish Camp built by the Edwards family had seating for 225 people. That restaurant burned down in 1968. The family decided to rebuild constructing a bigger place adjacent to the original site. Though there is now seating capacity for 554, the place fills up by 6:00 PM on weekends. In fact, there is often a wait. "We really couldn't handle any more people at one time than we do now," Phil says. "Our kitchen staff and waitresses have to go all out the way it is now." There are regulars from as far away as Columbia and Charlotte who come to dine on an almost weekly basis.

As you would imagine, seafood is the big draw at Catawba Fish Camp. There is a wide range of choices and most platters are all-you-can-eat. Hungry eaters can choose perch ($6.25), catfish ($7.95), flounder ($7.95), shrimp ($7.50), or black bass ($6.95) and eat as much as their hearts desire. Platters come with fries or baked potato, hush puppies, and coleslaw. "Some people tell us they come more for the hush puppies and slaw than they do for the seafood," Phil says.

Although some platters are not all-you-can-eat, the manager explains that you get so much you wouldn't ask for more if you could. These include the seafood platter ($9.50), scallops ($8.75), crab legs ($9.00), deviled crabs ($5.50), and fantail shrimp ($7.75). For non-seafood eaters there are several chicken dishes.

The restaurant is open to the public Wednesday through Saturday. On Tuesday nights the place is often used for private functions. Three rooms in the back of the building are large enough to handle three separate parties at once or they can be opened up for one big party. "We host some functions like the Gamecock Club here because it is the only place big enough in the area to accommodate that many people," declares Phil.

After one visit to the Catawba Fish Camp you will understand why it has remained in business for almost half a century.

Summerton Diner

Owner or manager:	Lynnelle Blackwell
Address:	US 301, Summerton
Directions:	From I-95, take exit 108 N 1 mi. to US 301/ US 15. Follow US 301/US 15 N approx. 1 mi. Restaurant is first building in town, on left.
Phone number:	803-485-6835
Hours of operation:	MON–WED 7:00AM–9:00PM, FRI–SUN 6:00AM–9:30PM
Payment method:	local checks
Reservations:	not accepted
Dress:	casual
Gratuity:	not included
Bar:	no
Alcohol:	not served
Diet/light menu:	broiled seafood
Children's menu:	no
Average price for meal:	$8.00
Discounts:	none offered
Catering:	no
House favorites:	chicken and dumplings, seafood
Other:	closed on Thursdays

In 1967, John Hughes left the Navy, where he served as cook, and he and wife Lois purchased the Summerton Diner. That was during a time when US Hwy. 301 was the major route for people traveling between the North and Florida. Summerton is, in fact, the halfway point between New York City and Miami. Because of the constant stream of traffic, the restaurant flourished.

Just after John and Lois made their purchase, a major event happened: I-95 opened, just three miles outside town. Many of the other local restaurants began moving out to the interstate. John stayed put. According to Lynnelle Blackwell, the couple's daughter, "Everyone told my dad he better move or he will never make it. But he wouldn't even consider moving. He said if the diner provided good food, people would find it."

John was evidently a revolutionary thinker and the restaurant has become well-known throughout the state and beyond. *Southern Living*, *Sandlapper* Magazine, and the *Palm Beach News* have all written about this little establishment. And *Unlimited Magazine* recently named it one of the best diners in the country.

Lynnelle admits that she is constantly amazed at where her customers in this tiny town of 900 people come from. "A couple who are regulars here told me they were recently in Canada. They were in a McDonalds there and were wearing USC sweatshirts. The girl behind the counter began talking to them and asked if they had ever eaten at our restaurant; she said that her family drove to Florida every year and always made a point at stopping in Summerton to eat!"

The diner has remained an important part of the family. After John died, Lois took over running the restaurant. After a time, Lois remarried. Lynnelle began to help out when her mother and stepfather were away on vacation, all the while hoping she would one day get the opportunity to take over full-time.

That chance came in 1987. "My mother asked me if I wanted to run it. I wasn't sure if I could handle it, but I have surprised myself," Lynnelle exclaims.

In asking customers what their favorite dish is, the answers were as varied as the menu. Lunchtime specials include a meat (such as chicken and dumplings, catfish, or stuffed bell peppers), three vegetables, dessert, and tea for just $5.50. Dinner specials include the chicken ($6.50), steak ($6.50), and quail ($8.95), as well as a variety of seafood dishes. Lynnelle takes great pride in the preparation of her food. "We want people to think they have just eaten at grandma's table."

With its proximity to Lake Marion and I-95, many well-known people have enjoyed meals at the Summerton Diner. One of the most interesting people to dine there in recent years was someone with whom all South Carolinians are familiar: Tammy Faye Baker. "She came in with some businessmen. There was no doubt it was her," Lynelle said. "She had all the make-up on, the full works, including false eyelashes. Then after she finished eating, instead of putting on lipstick she put on mascara!"

The next time you are traveling on I-95 through Clarendon County, make your way over to Summerton Diner. It won't be hard to find—just follow the crowd.

♦ The peach is South Carolina's official state fruit.

Hoot's

Owner or manager:	Pat Douglas and Shannon Mills
Address:	128 S. Congress Street, Winnsboro
Directions:	US 321 runs through downtown Winnsboro, where it becomes Congress Street. Hoot's stands on Congress between Washington and Liberty Streets, across from First Union Bank.
Phone number:	803-635-6789
Hours of operation:	MON–FRI 7:00AM–2:00PM; DINNER HRS. VARY
Payment method:	checks
Reservations:	not needed, but accepted
Dress:	casual
Gratuity:	not included
Bar:	yes
Alcohol:	beer and wine only
Diet/light menu:	several diet and low cholesterol meals
Children's menu:	yes ($2.95)
Average price for meal:	$2.50, breakfast • $3.75, lunch or dinner
Discounts:	10% to seniors
Catering:	limited
House favorites:	pimento cheese sandwich, chicken salad
Other:	convenient to I-77

In the 1940s and 1950s, children in Winnsboro would run downtown after school to Colonial Drugstore. There, they would sit at the marble bar and order the drugstore's trademark dish: a pimento cheese sandwich.

The drugstore is gone, but the marble bar—made from blue marble mined in Winnsboro—is still being used in the restaurant that now occupies the building: Hoot's. Fortunately for Winnsboro residents, the establishment's owners, Pat Douglas and her daughter Shannon Mills, own the original pimento cheese recipe that is so loved. "The sandwiches are exactly the same as they were forty years ago," Pat claims.

In 1993, Pat and Shannon discussed how tired they both

were of their jobs. Not long after, Pat heard that Hoot's—her favorite restaurant in town—was on the market. The mother–daughter team wasted no time, quickly buying the place—though neither had ever worked in the restaurant business.

Inexperience doesn't seem to have made a difference, as Hoot's has remained a popular place in Winnsboro. While they originally opened only for breakfast and lunch, they have recently expanded and now serve dinner on Thursday and Friday evenings. Pat said she is so busy she wishes she could give up her breakfast business but is afraid it would offend too many people. She knows of one group she'd better not offend: the local clergy who meet there several mornings each week at the same table, now fondly known as "the preachers' table."

Countryside pictures and rustic plates adorn the walls of the homey restaurant, and the menu invites patrons to "come and enjoy a nice, quiet meal in a cozy, friendly atmosphere."

Pat runs the breakfast and lunch shifts; Shannon manages the evenings. Hoot's is in close proximity to the courthouse, and it isn't unusual to have judges and lawyers sitting in booths while Pat prepares take-out meals for juries.

The menu is very affordable. Breakfast is $2.50, with a choice of bacon, eggs, and grits or omelettes. Lunchtime offers a choice of salads (grilled chicken, the best seller, $4.25) and sandwiches (turkey, $3.75; croissants with roast beef, ham, or turkey, $3.95). Dinnertime favorites include the loaded potato (with ham, turkey, bacon, cheese, broccoli, and sour cream, served with a house salad, $6.95), and various chicken dishes and steaks. The Thursday night special is spaghetti, a dish so popular they usually sell out.

Senior citizens receive a 10% discount, and a children's menu is available (four choices, $2.95 each). There are even several low cholesterol and low calorie meals. For those with a sweet tooth, there is a "dessert of the day."

Whether you are a health conscious diner or someone with a hearty appetite, Hoot's has something that will fill your need without squeezing your wallet.

Hard Times Cafe

Owner or manager:	H. C. Robinson
Address:	US 1, Cassatt
Directions:	Cassatt is a tiny town NW of Camden. From intersection of US 521 & US 1 downtown, follow US 1 about 12 miles to town sign for Cassatt. Restaurant is on right, beside post office.
Phone number:	803-425-7308
Hours of operation:	MON–FRI BREAKFAST 8:00AM–10:30PM, LUNCH 11:00AM–2:00PM
Payment method:	checks
Reservations:	not needed
Dress:	casual
Gratuity:	not included
Bar:	no
Alcohol:	not served
Diet/light menu:	no
Children's menu:	child's plate available
Average price for meal:	buffet, $4.95
Discounts:	none offered
Catering:	yes
House favorites:	pork chops (THU), ribs (MON), banana pudding
Other:	buffet is all-you-can-eat

After retiring from the DuPont plant in Camden in 1992, H. C. Robinson decided he wanted to make a foray into the restaurant business. Coming up with a name for his new place was not difficult. "I decided that I have been through enough hard times in my life it might bring me good luck to name it Hard Times Cafe," he says.

The choice seems to have been a lucky one. The restaurant has thrived from the start, despite its out-of-the-way location. Situated in Cassatt, a tiny town about fourteen miles northeast of Camden, the restaurant stands beside the town's lone public building: the post office.

H. C. and his wife Annette run the establishment, which is truly a family affair. Workers include their daughter and H. C.'s mother and sister.

Hard Tmes started out selling only barbecue but expanded its fare. Annette says H. C. always wished there was a place in the area where he could get country homecooking. Since no other place existed, Hard Times changed its menu to satisfy H. C.'s tastes.

Annette accurately describes the restaurant's fare: "If you don't like your food flavored with fatback, don't come here!"

It's true. This is not the place for people counting fat grams or watching cholesterol. The focal point of the menu is the daily buffet. For $6, you can have as much as you want of three different meats, a variety of vegetables, hush puppies, coleslaw, dessert, and iced tea. The choices of meats and vegetables change daily. Thursday's special, pork chops, is prepared by H. C. on a grill behind the building. It's the most popular item of the week. Catfish lovers should go on Friday. Catfish strips and catfish stew are served. Fans of ribs need to dine on Mondays. One of the highlights of the buffet is the dessert section. Banana pudding and chocolate cream pudding are daily staples.

For those not hungry enough for the buffet, hamburgers ($1.75), grilled cheese sandwiches ($1.15), and cheeseburgers ($2.00) are available.

With only a small number of people living in Cassatt, the success of Hard Times stems from people making the drive on US Hwy. 1 from both Camden and Florence. Many people in the area are introduced to H. C.'s cooking through events he caters throughout the Midlands, such as hunting field trials.

With the town of Cassatt lacking sites and the restaurant located in a non-descript cinder block building, the food is the reason for visiting. Take a drive. You will agree that Hard Times Cafe is worth the journey.

Lucy's

Owner or manager:	Vint Partridge
Address:	1043 Broad Street, Camden
Directions:	From I-20, take US 521 (exit 98) N about 2 miles to downtown. Restaurant is on left, 2 blocks past Rutledge Street, just beyond US 1. Look for green and white awning. (US 521 is Broad Street downtown.)
Phone number:	803-432-9096
Hours of operation:	TUE–SAT 4:00–9:00PM
Payment method:	credit cards
Reservations:	recommended on weekends
Dress:	casual to formal
Gratuity:	not included
Bar:	yes
Alcohol:	yes
Diet/light menu:	several vegetarian dishes
Children's menu:	no
Average price for meal:	$17.95
Discounts:	none offered
Catering:	some in-house catering
House favorites:	oysters, ostrich, veal, filet mignon

When you walk into Lucy's in downtown Camden, you might think you're entering a dress shop. The left window contains a female mannequin and the right a male. The female mannequin is, in fact, Lucy, named for the mother-in-law of owner Vint Partridge. The male mannequin is Lucy's unnamed boyfriend.

While one expects to find gourmet dining in Columbia and Charleston, visitors to Camden may be surprised to find such fine food in a city its size. When Vint and his wife made plans to start an upscale dining establishment, they originally considered moving to *the big city*. But they believed, with Camden's wealthy populace, they could make a go of it without packing their bags. Their restaurant had crowds from day one and has not slowed down since.

The menu may appear pricey to some but its uniqueness will astonish and delight. There are few other places in the state that specialize in such entrees as ostrich (the chef's favorite, $19.95), New Zealand lamb rack ($18.95), and veal liver ($17.95).

The location was actually a clothing store prior to Vint's purchasing it. Plaster walls were removed to reveal soft red brick. The lowered ceiling was taken out and a tin ceiling was discovered above it, just waiting to be redone. The new owner's next step was to rip up the carpet and plywood. Underneath he discovered red wooden floors that had never been used. The entire project took almost seven months, with Vint doing much of the work himself.

Upon entering the place, your eye is drawn to the tremendous twenty-two-foot mahogany bar, which predates the Civil War. Originally the bar at the Williard Hotel in Philadelphia, it has quite a history to it. Walt Whitman is said to have written a poem about Yankee officers who spend all their time getting drunk at this particular bar instead of fighting Rebels. And, at least one former president is said to have had drinks at it. Vint first saw the bar at an antiques store up North years ago. It made such an impression on him he returned to purchase it when he decided to open Lucy's.

The restaurant's popularity has reached down to Columbia. The city's residents who take the thirty-five-minute drive to dine at Lucy's make up approximately forty percent of its customer base.

Dinner prices range from $16 to $20, but the choices are varied and well worth the price. One of the favored dinner entrees is oysters ($17.95), which chef James King prepares using four separate breadings. So that customers have a variety, half the menu changes every other week. Vegetarian and light dishes are available, as is a "catch of the day." The desserts are made fresh and change often.

The lunch menu is not quite as elaborate but still brings in a good crowd. Choices include salads (chicken, fried oyster, and artichoke, $5.50 to $7.50), veal livers ($7.95), eggs benedict ($7.25), pasta ($6.95), and po boy sandwiches ($6.50).

All dishes are prepared by James King, a certified chef who attended culinary schools in New York, Chicago, and Florida. While many customers are dressed somewhat formally, Vint points out that he wears jeans to the restaurant almost every day and encourages others to do so.

When you visit the restaurant, be sure to say hello to Lucy. Note what she's wearing. The staff changes her outfit once a week. Don't feel too bad for her anonymous boyfriend. He gets to join her in her window on New Year's Eve!

♦ The city of Camden is host each April to the Colonial Cup, an equestrian steeplechase that attracts thousands of spectators.

♦ South Carolina's last legal duel was fought in 1880.

The Paddock

Owner or manager:	Richard Cox and Robert Murphy
Address:	314 Rutledge Street, Camden
Directions:	From I-20, take US 521 (exit 98) N about 2 miles to Rutledge Street (2nd light) downtown. Turn right on Rutledge. Restaurant in first block, on left. (US 521 is Broad Street downtown.)
Phone number:	803-432-3222
Hours of operation:	TUE–SAT 11:00AM–10:00PM
Payment method:	local checks, major credit cards
Reservations:	accepted, but not needed
Dress:	casual to formal
Gratuity:	included for groups of 5 or more
Bar:	yes
Alcohol:	yes
Diet/light menu:	♥ noted beside menu items
Children's menu:	child's plate available
Average price for meal:	sandwiches, $4.75 • meals, $13.95
Discounts:	none offered
Catering:	limited
House favorites:	club sandwich, chicken dishes, prime rib
Other:	accoustic guitarist performs in bar on weekends; convenient to I-20

People familiar with Camden know its history with horse racing. The Carolina Cup in March and polo matches through-out the year make it one of the state's most popular equestrian towns. It is therefore only appropriate that a restaurant with a name like The Paddock be a favorite with town locals—as it has been since 1977. It was in that year ex-jockey Nick Butler from Ireland and Skipp Achnuff from Philadelphia purchased the building (which was used as a stable at one time) and turned it into a restaurant. The business has since sold to Rick Cox, Vanessa Cox, and Robert Murphy (Butler's nephew, also from Ireland).

"Since we do have an equestrian theme, we get all the horse people in here," Robert Murphy explains. "But almost everyone in Camden has been in at one time or another, not to mention the out-of-town traffic."

The menu is quite complete. Nine different salads are offered, including the Carolina Salad (with Julienne strips of grilled chicken breast, $5.95), which is the biggest seller. Sandwiches are also on the menu: prime rib ($6.95), corned beef ($4.75), hot pastrami ($4.75), and Italian sausage ($4.75). Dinner entrees include the very popular barbecue baby back ribs (rack, $12.95; half rack, $8.95), grilled chicken oscar (breasts topped with crabmeat and asparagus, $14.95), and linguine with clam sauce ($14.95). Prime rib au jus ($16.25) is served only on weekends and almost always sells out. Healthy choices are easy and abundant. Hearts are placed next to the names of low cholesterol dishes.

"There is not anything on our menu I would not recommend to someone," Robert declares. "We pride ourselves on everything we serve."

If you're just coming in to relax, the bar area has the feel of an English pub. There is live entertainment on Friday and Saturday nights, and patrons can order food from the bar.

The Paddock serves 100 to 150 people on weekends and reservations, though not required, are recommended.

The next time you're in the mood to talk about the chances of the three-year-old thoroughbreds in the upcoming Derby, a stop at The Paddock is in order.

Cogburn's

Owner or manager:	Ike Cogburn
Address:	1061 Sunset Blvd. (US 378), West Columbia
Directions:	From State House, follow Gervais Street W about 1 mile to Congaree River bridge (beside State Museum). Just after bridge, bear right onto US 378 (Sunset Blvd.); continue about 1-1/2 miles. Restaurant on left, beside Triangle Ice Co. [Cogburn's is about halfway between State House and I-26.]
Phone number:	803-791-4581
Hours of operation:	SUN–MON 6:30AM–2:00PM, TUE–SAT 6:30AM–9:30PM
Payment method:	checks, major credit cards
Reservations:	not needed
Dress:	casual
Gratuity:	not included
Bar:	no
Alcohol:	no
Diet/light menu:	no
Children's menu:	yes
Average price for meal:	$3.25, breakfast • $10.00 lunch/dinner
Discounts:	none offered
Catering:	no
House favorites:	steak sandwich, baked chicken
Other:	private group dining available

When is a steak sandwich not a steak sandwich? To answer that question, simply visit Cogburn's, a longtime favorite in the Midlands.

There are few area restaurants that can date themselves prior to D-Day, but this is one of them. It began its successful run in 1942 on Sumter Street in downtown Columbia. Ike Cogburn came into the business, which had been started by his older brother, in 1953 right out of high school. For years the place was drawing big crowds at the Sumter Street location, especially on Sundays when the line would stretch down the street.

"We've always been known as a family business, and that is who we still try to please," explains Ike, a throwback to another era himself with his tight crew cut. "We don't serve alcohol, and though it might cost us some business, most of our regulars already know it."

Since the beginning, the biggest seller on Cogburn's menu has been the Steak Sandwich. This is a nine-ounce steak served with a salad and a potato ($9.95). There is no sandwich involved at all. Ike explained how it got its name.

"It used to be that if any meal was served that included either a roll or bun, the meal was called a sandwich. It didn't have anything to do with what people call sandwiches today. The steak sandwich is what we called the dish when we first opened the place, and I just never saw a need to change it."

The menu offers a wide array of items including seafood (oysters, in season, and shrimp), hamburgers, salads, and omelettes. Ike has seen his selections change as the diets of his customers have.

"It used to be that some people would come in everyday and get a steak. Now everyone knows that will kill you, though it is okay to have one every once in a while. A few years ago I thought I would try serving grilled chicken to see how it went over. With people watching their cholesterol, it is now our second biggest seller."

Breakfast is another good time to try Cogburn's. For only $3.25 you can have two eggs, bacon or sausage, grits or hash browns, toast, and coffee. There are also five different omelettes to choose from ($3.25 each), all of which are available on the dinner menu as well. Ike says he hosts several church groups that make his place a regular stopping point for their breakfasts.

If you are a Gamecock (University of South Carolina) fan, you are definitely welcome at the restaurant—although they will also serve Tiger (Clemson University) fans. Ike is a big supporter of USC and even has his waitresses wear red and black as a show of support. Football coach Brad Scott often comes in to eat; he too chooses the steak sandwich on most occasions.

Ike moved the business away from downtown Columbia in 1979 after a dispute with the landlord. Most of his customers, he said, were willing to drive a few extra miles to stick with him. While he enjoys the business, he admits he couldn't do it without his wife's help.

"The restaurant business is a hard one to be in, and you need all the family help you can get. I've been lucky to have both my wife and son working with me for a long time. That's why we are truly a family restaurant."

♦ Number of South Carolinians who died in Vietnam: 980.
Number of South Carolinians who died fighting for the Confederacy: 12,922.

Flight Deck

Owner or manager:	Ted Stambolitis
Address:	109 Old Chapin Road, Lexington
Directions:	At intersection of US 378 and US 1, behind Eckerds (about 3 miles W of I-20).
Phone number:	803-957-5990
Hours of operation:	MON–THU 11:00AM–9:00PM, FRI 11:00AM–11:00PM, SAT 11:00AM–10:00PM
Payment method:	checks; major credit cards
Reservations:	not needed
Dress:	casual
Gratuity:	included for groups of 6 or more
Bar:	no
Alcohol:	beer and wine
Diet/light menu:	salads, light sandwiches
Children's menu:	no
Average price for meal:	$6.00
Discounts:	none offered
Catering:	no
House favorites:	all sandwiches and cheesecakes
Other:	terrific atmosphere

An interest in aviation is common among young people. Many children build model airplanes and fly remote controlled aircraft. For some, this fascination continues into adulthood and actually lead into flight.

Ted Stambolitis fits into that category. Since his boyhood he has studied airplanes and famous pilots. He earned his pilot's license as a teenager and began flying experimental aircraft. Unlike most kids who grow tired of their collections, Ted continued garnering aviation momentos.

Ted also has a second love: the restaurant business. In the early 1990s he made a decision that incorporated both his interests.

"I had been in the restaurant business for twenty years but

I had never been in a position to dictate the decorating of a place," he said. "Finally, I got the chance to open a place where I would have control over how it would look. I knew that I wanted to combine my love of restaurants with my love for aviation."

Thus was born Flight Deck, a popular dining establishment known for its sandwiches and Greek dinners. From the name alone you can guess the restaurant's theme. Upon opening the door, it would be easy to believe you have walked into the state's aviation museum instead of a restaurant. Every inch of wall space is covered with pictures, photographs, awards, and insignia. Equally impressive is the number of models that hang from the ceiling. Ted tells how it all came about: "I put up all the pictures of airplanes I had collected through the years as well as a few of the models. I was amazed how well they went over and how people really were interested in them. Soon friends, strangers, and veterans started bringing me items they had. They said it would be an honor if I would display them at the Flight Deck. I always say yes. I'm actually the one who is honored that they would want me to have these things."

Ted has garnered so many items he has only room for about 300 permanent pieces. He has an additional 150 pictures in the back he rotates on display. He especially likes airplanes from World War II and is proud of the many pictures that veterans have given him. People in the aviation community have learned about his place and visit when they are in the area.

"Bob Morgan of the *Memphis Belle* [a famous WWII bomber that has been the subject of at least one movie] has been in. Thomas Thain [a pilot who gained notoriety by shooting down a German jet from his propellor-power plane] gave me a large picture with his name on it. We also got an autograph from Jimmy Doolittle [who led the first bombing raids on Japan] when he came to Columbia."

Even if you are not into aircraft, the food is reason enough to visit this bistro. There is a great variety: Greek dinners, sandwiches, Mexican dishes, Philly cheese steaks, ribs, pizza, and fresh cooked burgers, just to name a few. Many people pick from a selection of over twenty sandwiches, which have such names as the Flying Fortress, the Spruce Goose, and the Tailgunner. Most sandwiches cost around $5.

No matter what you decide to get, make sure you leave room for dessert. Ted serves about ten different styles of home-made cheesecakes, all of them big sellers. With choices such as Oreo, Snickers, amaretto, and Heath Bar, you might just skip the entree and go straight to dessert.

When next dining out, make plans to *land* at Flight Deck. You'll be pleased with your final destination.

♦ Gen. Jimmy Doolittle trained for his 1942 raid on Tokyo at what is now the Columbia Metropolitan Airport.

♦ The Lexington County town of Irmo hosts the annual Okra Festival.

Sub Cabin

Owner or manager:	Frank Keck and Lee McLaughlin
Address:	1028 Sunset Blvd., West Columbia
Directions:	From State House, follow Gervais St. W about 1 mi. to Congaree River bridge (beside State Museum). Just after bridge, bear right onto US 378 (Sunset Blvd.) and continue about 1-1/2 mi. Restaurant on right, just past Craft St. Look carefully. It sits far off road and is not easily seen. [Sub Cabin is about halfway between State House and I-26.]
Phone number:	803-796-7827
Hours of operation:	MON–THU 11:00AM–10:00PM FRI–SAT 11:00AM–11:00PM
Payment method:	checks, major credit cards
Reservations:	not needed
Dress:	casual
Gratuity:	not included
Bar:	no
Alcohol:	beer and wine
Diet/light menu:	salads
Children's menu:	yes
Average price for meal:	$5.00
Discounts:	none offered
Catering:	yes
House favorites:	buffalo wings, Philly cheese steak
Other:	unique building and location

Do you think a couple brothers from Philadelphia could be successful if they moved down to South Carolina and opened up a restaurant that served as its specialty a dish well-known to Yankees but unknown in Dixie? No need to answer that question. Frank Keck and Lee McLaughlin have already accomplished that feat with the Sub Cabin in West Columbia.

The brothers grew up in the Philadelphia suburb of West Chester. Lee moved to South Carolina in the '70s and worked as manager of several restaurants in the state. Frank followed him down in 1981 and took a job with an advertising firm. One day the two talked and decided they wanted to take a shot together at the restaurant business.

"Lee and I were both tired of working for other people," Frank explains. "I had worked for Marriott previously so we both knew about the restaurant business. We decided not to do anything too big, just something that we could make a living on."

That was in 1982. They began looking for a facility to house their new, unnamed restaurant. They found a vacant building—actually a log cabin—that had previously been a restaurant. It was small and cozy, but the real reason they chose it, according to Frank, is, "the price was right."

When it came to deciding what food they would offer, the brothers never considered serving traditional southern cooking. "We decided we would serve the kind of food we liked and grew up with," Frank says. "The thing Philadelphia is best known for is the Philly cheese steak. We checked around, and there wasn't any place that served a real cheese steak. The other thing Lee and I decided to put on the menu was chicken wings. At that time only one other restaurant in town served wings. Most people down here had never heard of buffalo wings and weren't sure what they were."

After fifteen years and thousands of pounds of chicken wings later, there aren't many people in the Columbia area who haven't tried the Sub Cabin's wings. Initially offered in hot, medium, and mild, the wings are now available in seven different styles including Oriental and teriyaki.

As for the Philly cheese steak, that too has caught on quite well. "The cheese steak is definitely our number one item," Frank said, adding that it was also his personal favorite. "We use a special cut of meat, and it's just like one you would get up North."

Besides the cheese steak and chicken wings, there are other sandwiches and subs on the menu. The place draws its largest crowds at lunch, and it is common to see lawyers in suits waiting beside muddy-booted construction workers. In case you wonder why there is a bottle of vinegar on all the tables, just remember that the owners want their customers to have a "fair" experience.

"We offer homemade sliced fries. Some people call them homemade potato chips," Frank said. "They are like the ones you can get at the fair. Since people always enjoy putting vinegar on them at the fair, we decided to offer the same opportunity at the Sub Cabin. The only thing is that some people put the vinegar on all their food!"

One of the most appealing things about the restaurant is the log cabin itself. Although Frank describes it as "shabby," it's what the rest of us might call rustic. The brothers have expanded their building twice but still have seating for only about eighty. Frank says they may be seeking a new location in the next few years, but is concerned that in the move they "might lose some customers."

Even if you are a staunch Rebel, you should check out the Sub Cabin. You don't have to be a Yankee to like the food.

♦ Divorce was not legalized in South Carolina until 1949.

A Locals' Guide

Perry's
Back Porch

Owner or manager:	John Perry
Address:	Main Street, Prosperity
Directions:	Prosperity is a small town about 6 mi. SE of Newberry (and 5 mi. W of I-26). US 76 runs through Prosperity; Main St. runs parallel for a few blocks. Restaurant is on Main beside town gazebo.
Phone number:	803-364-3556
Hours of operation:	TUE–SAT 11:00AM–3:00PM, 5:00–8:00PM
Payment method:	checks
Reservations:	not needed
Dress:	casual
Gratuity:	not included
Bar:	no
Alcohol:	not served
Diet/light menu:	salads
Children's menu:	no
Average price for meal:	$4.50
Discounts:	none offered
Catering:	in-house only
House favorites:	fried and baked chicken, any dessert
Other:	carry-out available from in-house bakery

When asked how it was a man who had spent his entire life working in the furniture manufacturing business decided to open a restaurant, John Perry had a simple answer: he couldn't find any place to eat.

John Perry, owner of Perry's Back Porch, explained what happened in 1979. "I was going to open my own small manufacturing facility and was living near Prosperity at the time. My wife and I decided to go into town one day to eat and found that there wasn't any place. It didn't take too long for me to realize that I might want to change my business plans."

Fortunate for his customers, John altered his course and opened a restaurant on the town square in Prosperity. The business has grown over the years from one building to two and includes a bakery and gift shop. While the place may be unknown to many in the Palmetto State, it has become a popular stop for travelers from the Buckeye State.

"We try to meet the people who come in here, and we noticed that all of a sudden we started getting a lot of guests from Ohio. After a month of this, my curiosity got to me and I asked one of them how they happened to hear about the place. They said they had read an article in their local paper by a noted food critic in Toledo—an article I didn't even know about!"

After dining at Perry's Back Porch, you can see why it's a popular stop. The food is served cafeteria style, with most entrees priced at $1.95, vegetables at 75 cents, and salads at 85 cents. There are also desserts and bread, homemade and well worth the money. The choices change regularly, according to season, as John tries to serve as many fresh items as possible.

While the food is outstanding, your visit must include

meeting Betty Dominick. John says Betty, the unofficial welcoming committee for both the restaurant and the town of Prosperity, is the key to the operation. "She's a real people person and I let her do her own thing. If she doesn't know you before you come, she'll make a point to get to know you before you leave," he says.

Sunday is the busiest day at the Back Porch, with the line routinely stretching out the door. Many customers make the twenty-five-mile drive from Chapin and Irmo. John closes the place on Mondays; this led to an interesting meeting one day.

The owner was at the restaurant checking on things one Monday when a man popped his head in the door. John explained that they were closed. The visitor was quite disappointed, as he had driven, he said, from Beaufort to meet a friend at the restaurant. John offered the stranger something to drink while he waited for his friend and struck up a conversation. After talking for some time, John stuck out his hand and introduced himself. The visitor shook John's hand and introduced himself as well. The unfortunate customer was Pat Conroy (famed South Carolina author of *The Lords of Discipline* and *The Prince of Tides*).

While there are some items on the menu that are low in calories and fat, this is a place that you should go when you are not counting fat grams. The fried chicken, chicken livers, and country fried steak are big sellers.

Those who don't want to wait to be served can go to the bakery section and get take-out. Be sure to look around this room. It was formerly the town post office and still has the antique post office boxes.

The back dining room may be rented for private parties. This room is also worth noting. Its soft red brick walls date back 100 years.

It seems appropriate that the prosperous Back Porch is located in a town called Prosperity. Given the town's close proximity to I-26, Perry's Back Porch is a good stopping point on any trip.

Ruff Brothers

Owner or manager:	Bo and Henry Ruff
Address:	3754 SC 219, Newberry
Directions:	From I-26, take SC 219 (exit 76) E approx. 4 miles. The restaurant, which looks like an old Esso gas station, is on the right.
Phone number:	803-276-9213
Hours of operation:	TUE–SAT 8:30AM–7:30PM
Payment method:	checks
Reservations:	not needed
Dress:	casual
Gratuity:	not included
Bar:	no
Alcohol:	beer
Diet/light menu:	grilled chicken breast
Children's menu:	no
Average price for meal:	$7.00
Discounts:	none offered
Catering:	yes
House favorites:	ribs, catfish

Brothers often make great teams! The Van Dyke brothers are known for comedy, the Kennedy brothers for politics. In Newberry, two brothers are making names for themselves with good food.

Bo and Henry Ruff, who could be pictured in the dictionary beside the phrase "good ol' boys," run Ruff Brothers restaurant. Although located in a rural setting, it isn't unusual for customers to have a lengthy wait on weekends. The success of the restaurant is surprising considering the brothers' background.

Bo, self-proclaimed leader of the pair, explained how they got started. "I quit a construction job and was looking for something to do. Henry had always worked with me, and we decided to try a restaurant. We had never been in that business before but had done a little cooking around the house. So far it seems to have worked out."

Their first step was to find a location. The brothers had grown up in a small community about ten miles outside the town of Newberry. One of the only commercial buidlings in the area was an old Esso gas station and general store, built in 1923, that had been closed down for a number of years. The building looks like one out of a Norman Rockwell painting from the '40s. The siblings wanted to be located close to home so they bought the place. Before long, Ruff Brothers restaurant opened up.

When traveling toward the restaurant on SC Hwy. 219, you will be tempted several times to turn around, convinced that you are going the wrong way. Out past farmland and woods, the former gas station eventually appears.

Inside, the place has retained much of its original construction. Old pine beams still hold up the roof and the walls are of pine boards. A long counter separates the kitchen from the dining area. Ceiling fans stir the air, distributing the delicious smells from the kitchen, whetting customers' appetites. The place is decorated with a collection of stuffed ducks, and fish and deer antlers hang on the wall.

One quick gaze around the restaurant will tell you what the house specialties are: catfish and ribs. Bones pile up on tables faster than pickup trucks pile up outside. The ribs ($7.49) are marinated and slow cooked, and the catfish ($5.99 to $9.49, depending on amount) is fried to perfection. If these items don't tempt you, there are other choices, such as the seafood platter ($11.99), barbecue chicken ($5.89), steak fingers ($5.19), and frog legs ($9.99). You can watch as the Ruffs work behind the counter preparing the food. It's obvious they enjoy their work.

The heart of the customer base comes from the local area. It isn't unusual for people to mill around among the tables visiting with friends.

The atmosphere of this eating establishment is old-timey and, if you stay long enough, you may forget what decade you're in. In keeping with the spirit of the old general store, the Ruffs also sell a variety of goods, such as cigarettes, beer, snuff, and candy, at the counter.

A visit to Ruff Brothers can best be described as "a little country in the country."

♦ Prior to 1870, the Newberry County town of Prosperity was called Frog Level.

Chef's Choice Steakhouse

Owner or manager:	Dan Bell
Address:	12757 Old Number 6 Hwy., Eutawville
Directions:	From I-95, take SC 6 (exit 98) SE (away from Santee) about 10 miles to SC 45 (downtown). Follow SC 45 (Old Number 6) W approx. 2 miles. Restaurant is on left side. (Eutawville is only a couple miles S of Lake Marion.)
Phone number:	803-494-3410
Hours of operation:	THU–SAT 5:30–11:00PM
Payment method:	checks, major credit cards
Reservations:	required for large groups
Dress:	casual
Gratuity:	not included
Bar:	no
Alcohol:	beer and wine
Diet/light menu:	no
Children's menu:	hamburger steak
Average price for meal:	$14.00
Discounts:	none offered
Catering:	in-house only
House favorites:	grilled steaks
Other:	fun place for large groups

For twenty-eight years Dan Bell ran Bell's Marina on Lake Marion, a full-service marina with a restaurant. He owned a large building a few miles away, near Eutawville, that he used as a boat showroom. When he decided to build a showroom at his marina, he no longer needed the Eutawville location. "I tried to sell it," he said, "but nobody wanted to buy."

After careful consideration, he made a decision: since he had experience in the restaurant industry and couldn't "unload" the building, he'd open a new restaurant. Thus was born Chef's Choice, well-known to anglers who visit Lake Marion.

The Eutawville restaurant is rustic in appearance. Much of

it is constructed of timbers recovered from an 1815 barn. Old farm equipment and kitchen utensils adorn the walls.

When you enter Chef's Choice, the first thing you notice is the enormous grill. Measuring four by twelve feet, it is large enough to cook 100 steaks at a time. With a grill this size, it doesn't take long to figure out the specialty of the house. Dan's huge kitchen glistens with stainless steel and porcelain, so it's ironic that about the only cooking done in there is baking potatoes.)

At some steak houses you worry about getting a good cut of beef. If you are unhappy with what you're served at Chef's Choice, you can only blame yourself. You choose your own steak—filet, ribeye, strip, or T-bone—from a refrigerated display case in the dining room. Prices range from $14.95 for a small to $16.95 for a large. Chicken breast, skewer shrimp, and scallops are also offered, but most customers come in for the basic steak dinner: steak, baked potato, and salad.

If you are one of those people who is never pleased with how the chef cooks your steak, *you* can do it. "In the beginning," Dan says, "people cooked a lot of their own steaks themselves. Most of them have found it's easier to let us do the work while they sit back and relax." On Friday and Saturday, if you let the staff do the cooking, you can enjoy your salad, which you prepare from a thirty-item salad bar, while listening to a live band.

The main dining room has seating for 125 people and the private party room can hold fifty. Most tables remain full on weekends—a significant accomplishment for a restaurant located in a town of only 350 people. So where do the customers come from? Dan, who is a member of a committee promoting the Lake Marion area, goes to travel shows all over the country. While making his presentation, he has been known to slip in a plug for his restaurant. His guest book includes signatures of visitors from South Africa, Japan, Russia, and across the U.S.

When you next decide to go fishing on Lake Marion, don't worry if you don't catch anything. Chef's Choice will make sure you don't go to bed hungry.

Chestnut Grill

Owner or manager:	Jim Albergotti
Address:	1455 Chestnut Street, Orangeburg
Directions:	From intersection of US 601 and US 21/US 178 BYPASS (Chestnut), follow Chestnut N about 1 mile (third traffic light). Restaurant is on left, across from K-Mart. (Convenient to I-26 and US 301.)
Phone number:	803-531-1747
Hours of operation:	MON–THU 11:00AM–9:30PM, FRI–SAT 11:00AM–10:00PM, SUN 11:00AM–9:00PM
Payment method:	major credit cards
Reservations:	not needed
Dress:	casual
Gratuity:	not included
Bar:	no
Alcohol:	beer and wine
Diet/light menu:	broiled items, seafood
Children's menu:	yes
Average price for meal:	$8.00
Discounts:	none offered
Catering:	no
House favorites:	chicken salad croissant, turkey club, Awesome Onion
Other:	carry-out available

Building a restaurant and building a restaurant business are two very different endeavors. If you don't believe it, ask Jim Albergotti. He's done both of them. Jim's original occupation was general contractor. In 1987 he built a restaurant, Mr. Steak, for his sons to run.

"None of us had any restaurant experience, so we were originally affiliated with a franchise out of Denver," Jim explained. This franchise, he said, supplied new owners with recipes, food, and cost-cutting methods of operation. Soon, however, the family realized there were some problems.

"It wasn't working. The people in Denver didn't know anything about what people in Orangeburg wanted," he said. Believing he could be of help, Jim left the construction business and joined his sons full-time at the restaurant as chief chef. "I had never really cooked before, other than helping out my wife," he said. "When you're raising three boys, cooking is sort of a family affair." .

Several local women donated recipes that were proven palate pleasers. The franchise's cost-cutting methods were scrapped. "For instance," Jim said, "the franchise used frozen, pre-breaded seafood. We now use all fresh seafood and do the breading by hand. It makes an incredible difference, although it isn't as cheap and fast as the franchise method." Jim also cuts his own steaks daily, which retains more of the natural flavor and moisture. This practice did not fit in with the franchise's recommendations either.

The menu at Chestnut Grill changes occasionally, though certain items remain constant. "We offer liver and onions. The staff hates to cook it but we have a following of people who come here because we serve it," Jim said.

Seafood and steaks are the big items. Among the seafood dishes are grilled salmon ($8.99), flounder ($9.99), deep fried scallops ($11.99), seafood casserole ($10.99), and a seafood platter ($11.99). Steaks include peppercorn strip ($8.99), ribeye ($13.99), New York strip ($12.99), and filet mignon ($15.99).

The lunch menu includes a variety of salads, sandwiches, and meals. Favorites include the barbecue baby back ribs ($7.99), steak tips ($5.99), charbroiled pork ($5.99), and the lunch sirloin ($6.99).

Many people go in just for the Awesome Onion ($4.99; small, $3.99), a super-sized flowered onion, battered, deep fried, and served with a spicy dipping sauce.

Since the restaurant's opening, Jim's eldest son has left to work with a food distributor. The middle son, Jack, earned a degree in hotel and restaurant management and now serves as manager of the facility while Jim works in the kitchen.

Andy's Deli

Owner or manager:	Andy Shlon
Address:	2005 Greene Street, Columbia
Directions:	From State House, follow Gervais Street E about 8 blocks to Harden Street. Turn right onto Harden and continue to second traffic light (Greene Street). Turn right onto Greene; Andy's is in first block, on the right.
Phone number:	803-799-ANDY
Hours of operation:	MON–SAT 10:00AM–9:00PM
Payment method:	checks
Reservations:	not needed
Dress:	casual
Gratuity:	not included
Bar:	no
Alcohol:	draft beer
Diet/light menu:	salads
Children's menu:	no
Average price for meal:	$4.49 (sandwich)
Discounts:	none offered
Catering:	no
House favorites:	Andy's Special, Rocket
Other:	a must for Gamecock fans!

Near the corner of Greene and Harden Streets in the Five Points section of Columbia stands a restaurant that has long been a favorite of USC students, fans, and alumni. That place is Andy's Deli. But, as good as the food is, much of the deli's popularity is due to the outgoing owner, Andy Shlon.

It would be hard not to recognize the restaurant's proprietor. He is the one taking orders behind the counter and greeting customers with "Hello, my friend" (to males) and "Hello, my dear" (to females). After more than twenty years of working his counter, Andy has become a Columbia landmark. Had it not been for a poor job market, however, none of this would have come about.

"I was part owner of Groucho's [Deli] and decided to leave," Andy explained. "I started looking around for another job, and it got so bad I was willing to take anything just to make money. Finally my lawyers convinced me to open my own place. So I started Andy's."

He took over an old Lum's restaurant building, opening his doors for business August 28, 1978. Andy's soon became a popular hangout with USC students, especially the cheerleaders. Photographs of past squads adorn the restaurant's walls, and each August they have their initial meeting of the season at Andy's. The owner displays lots of USC memorabilia and continues to support the school, which has provided him with so many customers through the years.

Andy's menu consists primarily of sandwiches and salads, and, like the decor, the prices have not changed much in twenty years. The top choice is Andy's Special, a combination of roast beef, turkey, Swiss cheese, and bacon bits ($4.49). The Rocket (roast beef, ham, and Swiss, $4.49) and the Astronaut (ham, turkey, and Swiss, $4.49) are also big sellers. If you are watching your waistline, you might consider My Friend's Salad Bowl (vegetarian, $2.55) or My Dear's Salad Bowl ($3.55).

If you enjoy cooking Mediterranean or Middle Eastern dishes at home, Andy's is the place to buy your supplies. Such rarities as fava beans, grape leaves, muenster cheese, and Lebanese bologna are available at Andy's.

Andy grew up in Beirut, Lebanon, where he attended the American University and became friends with several classmates from Columbia. Upon graduating, he worked for an airline. After several years, he came to the U.S. to visit his college buddies. Finding the South Carolina capital city very much to his liking, he decided to make it his home.

Unlike most people his age, Andy has no plans to retire. "Being around all the kids keeps me young," he says. "As long as I can stand up at the counter, I'll be here."

Blue Marlin
Seafood Kitchen

Owner or manager:	Jim Beach
Address:	1200 Lincoln Street, Columbia
Directions:	From State House, follow Grevais St. (US 1) W about 3 blocks to Lincoln St. Turn right onto Lincoln; restaurant is on right in first block, beside RR tracks.
Phone number:	803-799-3838
Hours of operation:	MON–FRI 11:30AM–2:00PM, 5:00–10:00PM SAT–SUN 5:00–10:00PM
Payment method:	major credit cards
Reservations:	not accepted
Dress:	casual to dressy
Gratuity:	not included
Bar:	yes
Alcohol:	yes
Diet/light menu:	several light choices available
Children's menu:	yes
Average price for meal:	$12.95
Discounts:	none offered
Catering:	no
House favorites:	shrimp and grits, fish, steaks
Other:	excellent location in Congaree Vista

For years people living in the state capital were forced to make a two-hour drive to the coast whenever they felt a craving for fresh Low Country seafood. That trip is no longer a necessity because of Blue Marlin Seafood Kitchen, which offers the Midlands "The Taste of the Southern Low Country."

New Jersey native and managing owner Jim Beach was running Longhorns Steakhouse in Columbia when he approached Bill Dukes about their opening a new restaurant together. It didn't take long for the two to come to an agreement.

"My partner and I wanted to have a place with a real South Carolina identity, food that people associated with this state," Jim said. "The most obvious choice is the food that is served throughout the Charleston area. We believed that this style would be a popular choice in Columbia."

Evidently their decision was a good one.

Located in the Congaree Vista, between the State Capitol and the State Museum, the restaurant occupies a building that was once a train station (which visitors will recognize immediately). After extensive renovations, Blue Marlin shines with sophistication. Music of the '30s and '40s fill the establishment, whose walls are adorned with photographs of fishermen with their catch.

It seems appropriate that the house specialty is shrimp and grits, a Charleston favorite, served with Cajun-spiced Andoville sausage and tasso gravy ($9.75). Jim's favorite is the oyster skillet bienville (oysters in shrimp sauce, served with grits, $11.75). If pasta is what you have in mind, there are several choices, including shrimp alfredo ($10.75) and shrimp scampi linquine ($10.95). For those not in a seafood mood, there are other excellent offerings. Pasta and chicken dishes are available, and the owner prides himself on his steaks.

If you are a fan of USC basketball, you might want to visit before one of their home games. The Gamecock players have their pregame meal at Blue Marlin. And, according to Jim, the restaurant provides the food for the "Monday After the Masters" celebrity golf tournament in Columbia, sponsored by Hootie and the Blowfish.

The managing owner began his career washing pots and pans at a restaurant on the Rhode Island coast during summer breaks from college. After graduation, he attended Johnson and Wales Culinary School in Rhode Island before working for Marriott Hotel in their food and beverage division. It was Marriott who brought him to the Columbia area to work for six months. Jim found he liked the city, and when Marriott notified him they were transferring him again, he decided to quit. He has never regretted that decision.

"The job is demanding and takes a lot of time and effort," Jim says, "but I feel it's worthwhile. All of our recipes are from scratch, and we are always trying new things. This business is one that you either love or hate, and luckily I love it."

♦ The Congaree Vista, now home to upscale shops and eateries, was once primarily a warehouse district.

Devine Foods

Owner or manager:	Angelo and Georgia Trifos
Address:	2702 Devine Street, Columbia
Directions:	From State House, take Gervais Street E about 8 blocks to Harden Street. Follow Harden to Devine Street (third traffic light). Turn left onto Devine; go about half mile to Woodrow Street. Restaurant is on right, corner of Devine and Woodrow.
Phone number:	803-252-0356
Hours of operation:	MON–SAT 11:00AM–9:00PM
Payment method:	local checks, major credit cards
Reservations:	not accepted
Dress:	casual
Gratuity:	not included
Bar:	no
Alcohol:	beer and wine
Diet/light menu:	grilled chicken, vegetable lasagna
Children's menu:	grilled chesse sandwich
Average price for meal:	$6.00
Discounts:	none offered
Catering:	yes
House favorites:	spanakopita, pastichio, lasagna
Other:	take-out available

Coming from families who were in the restaurant business, both Angelo and Georgia Trifos believed they could make it when they decided to open their own place, Devine Foods, in 1987. Little did they realize how quickly success would come.

"We didn't have the money to do any advertising, so we knew it would be slow the first year," Georgia says. "However, after a month or so people really started coming in. The word got around quickly. After ten years we still haven't needed to do any advertising."

The success of the restaurant seems amazing considering its location. Devine is one of five streets that converge to form Five Points, a popular shopping area filled with restaurants and bars. Devine Foods is located about a mile east of Five Points, nestled among specialty shops and old homes.

Georgia, originally from Canada, grew up in the restaurant business but was a practicing nurse at the time she and Angelo decided to start up the restaurant. Angelo had been in the restaurant industry for some time and served as a chef for Canadian Railways. They decided their restaurant would offer selections from Angelo's native home, Greece.

"Originally we were going to be primarily a take-out place and do some catering," Georgia says. "The building we have is somewhat small, but the dine-in business picked up so fast we decided to stick with it."

The kitchen opens onto the main dining area, allowing you to see your food being prepared. The room is filled with small tables, and pictures of Greece adorn the white walls. The place has the feel of a foreign cafe. A porch was added to the original structure to accommodate more customers.

Angelo and Georgia pride themselves on providing fresh

food prepared daily. According to Georgia, the spanakopita, a casserole with spinach, feta cheese, and green onions, is the restaurant's most popular dish ($4.75). The vegetable lasagna, made with broccoli, spinach, and a variety of spices, is another big seller ($4.75). "Some people come in and want the recipe for the vegetable lasagna," she says, "but it is just something we came up with."

Other items from the menu include roasted Greek-style chicken ($6.75), beef kabob ($8.75), the gyro ($4.25), and beef wrap on pita ($4.25). Many of these dishes come with a Greek salad.

"We also do daily specials," Georgia says, "and some customers will call up to see if lamb shanks are being offered."

Don't leave without trying the desserts. They are out of this world. They are so popular, in fact, other restaurants ask to buy them to resell at their own places.

It's a good thing Georgia and Angelo don't mind hard work and long hours. In addition to in-house dining at lunch and dinner, Devine Foods offers catering and take-out orders. It gets hectic but the couple enjoy the life.

How do customers feel about Devine Foods? Just ask them.

After visiting the place once, you too will quickly tell others about it.

Rockaways
Athletic Club

Owner or manager: Forest Whitlark, Paul Whitlark, and David
Nelson
Address: 2719 Rosewood Dr., Columbia
Directions: From State House, take Assembly Street S
about 2 miles to Rosewood Drive (state
fairgrounds on right). Turn left onto
Rosewood and continue about 2 miles.
Restaurant is on left, at Woodrow Street.
Gravel parking area.
Phone number: 803-256-1075
Hours of operation: MON–SAT 11:00AM–10:00PM
Payment method: local checks, major credit cards
Reservations: not accepted
Dress: casual
Gratuity: not included
Bar: yes
Alcohol: yes
Diet/light menu: salads
Children's menu: no
Average price for meal: burgers, $5.00 • specials, $8.00
Discounts: none offered
Catering: no
House favorites: Rockaways burger
Other: unique building and location

Many restaurants spend thousands upon thousands of
dollars to have a bright, huge sign proclaiming its name for all
to see. If you want to go to Rockaways Athletic Club, you'd
better get good directions. It doesn't have a sign, and the windows are tinted black.

Rockaways is owned by the trio of Forest Whitlark, Paul
Whitlark, and David Nelson. The place had been a neighborhood bar when the three of them took it over in the early
1980s, and they planned to keep it small and intimate. The
place didn't have a sign out front at the time they bought it,

and the new owners didn't see any need to change that.

"I don't know why there wasn't a sign," Forest said, "but I've always believed that the best advertising is word of mouth. We knew that if people liked the place, they would find it."

In the beginning the owners didn't plan to serve food, but they discovered if they had a kitchen on the premises it was much easier to get a mini-bottle license. So they added a kitchen.

"Once we put a kitchen in," Forest says, "we decided that we might as well use it. There wasn't any point in it just sitting there."

They began serving hamburgers. That caught on and soon people were flocking to the bar for the food as much as for the alcohol. The Rockaways burger, a hamburger covered with pimento cheese, ($3.75) became a big hit. Though it may sound like an odd combination, it is outstanding. Knowing that people love cheese, a variety of cheeseburgers hit the menu including blue, Swiss, cheddar, provolone, Monterey jack, feta, mozzarella, and gouda ($3.75 each). If you can't decide on just one cheese, you can get a combination.

"People really go crazy about the burgers," Forest said. "In 1994, *Southern Living* featured us in an article about the best burgers in the South."

Hamburgers are not the only thing on the menu, though. David grew up in the Cajun section of Louisiana. In 1983 he decided it would be fun to have a crawfish festival in the back parking lot. The festival has become an annual event and Rockaways now offers a number of Cajun seafood specials in the evening.

Other menu choices include chicken wings, sandwiches, soups, and steaks. Monday night is a very big night—shrimp and oysters are twenty-five cents each. And no matter what you choose from the menu, you must include an order of pimento cheese fries.

Rockaways's interior is a hodgepodge of spaces and textures. There are four dining rooms, three of them with bars. Walls are decorated with everything from Mardi Gras posters to an old American flag. When you visit, take a stroll through every room before deciding on a table, as each has its own unique atmosphere.

Though the name of the place implies otherwise, don't expect to find anyone at Rockaways Athletic Club doing anything particularly good for their body. How did the name come about? That remains a secret.

The clientele of Rockaways is a mix of businessmen, college students, and local residents. Once you try the place, you'll understand why the building doesn't need a sign.

♦ The members of the rock band Hootie and the Blowfish were students at the University of South Carolina in Columbia when the band formed.

Country Kitchen

Owner or manager:	Lisa Anderson
Address:	118 Hare Avenue, Saluda
Directions:	From intersection of US 378, US 178, and SC 39, head E on US 378 (Hare Ave.) 7/10ths mile. Restaurant is at corner of Hare and Travis Avenues, beside post office.
Phone number:	864-445-4643
Hours of operation:	MON–SAT 6:00–10:00AM, 11:00AM–2:00PM SUN 11:00AM–2:00PM
Payment method:	cash
Reservations:	not needed
Dress:	casual
Gratuity:	not included
Bar:	no
Alcohol:	not served
Diet/light menu:	salad
Children's menu:	no
Average price for meal:	$5.50, lunch • $6.50, dinner
Discounts:	none offered
Catering:	yes
House favorites:	fried chicken, Pollock fish

If you like country cooking and plenty of it, head for Country Kitchen in Saluda. The restaurant is managed by Lisa Anderson. Her parents, Mr. and Mrs. Fred Williams, and her sister, Krisey Williams, work right along beside her.

"We went into the restaurant business fifteen years ago. Then recently we moved to this location because we needed a bigger place," Lisa said.

The new building has a large dining area. Attached to this is an even bigger room where dances are held every Saturday night, beginning at nine o'clock. "There are two bands. They alternate every other weekend," she said.

There's plenty of room for catered affairs too, such as birthday parties and wedding rehearsal dinners. "We do all kinds of occasions either here or outside the restaurant," Lisa said.

Country Kitchen is well known locally for its lunch buffet. During the week, it offers three meats plus an assortment of vegetables and salads. On Sundays, there are generally four or five meats.

"We're really busy on Sundays, especially between noon and one because people come straight from church. We get packed and always have a line at that time," Lisa said.

The buffet ($5.50, weekdays; $6.50, weekends) is served from 11:00 AM to 2:00 PM and always includes fried chicken and Pollock fish. Other meats on the buffet may include chicken livers, country fried steak, peppered steak with onions and bell pepper, spare ribs, and barbeque. For vegetables you can select from okra, squash casserole, black-eyed peas, turnip greens, and butter beans. Macaroni and cheese is a daily staple. Also available are hush puppies, peach cobbler, and other Southern dishes you remember from Grandma's table.

If you're not real hungry or on a diet, you can order a sandwich or salad from the menu. Sandwiches include hamburger ($2.09), steak sandwich ($2.59), ham sandwich ($2.09), and Philly steak and cheese ($3.99). "That Philly steak sandwich is really delicious," Lisa said.

The breakfast menu includes cheese omelet with grits or hash browns, biscuit or toast, and coffee or tea ($3.99); one egg, bacon or sausage, also with grits or hash browns, biscuits or toast, and coffee or tea ($2.50); three pancakes, bacon or sausage ($3.75); and other traditional fare.

Lisa and her mother do the cooking. "Mom taught me real early to cook so I've been doing it most of my life. My sister isn't into it much, so she does the waitressing."

Riverside

AIKEN COUNTY
 Al's Family Restaurant (North Augusta)
 Country Connection (Burnettown)
 Variety Restaurant (Aiken)
ALLENDALE COUNTY
 Village Inn (Allendale)
BAMBERG COUNTY
 Denmark Diner (Denmark)
BARNWELL COUNTY
 Miller's Bread-Basket (Blackville)
 Winton Inn (Barnwell)
EDGEFIELD COUNTY
 Old McDonald Fish Camp (North Augusta)
 Ten Governors Cafe (Edgefield)
GREENWOOD COUNTY
 Blazers Restaurant (Greenwood)
 Rick's Uptown Cafeteria (Greenwood)
HAMPTON COUNTY
 Ernie's Restaurant (Hampton)
JASPER COUNTY
 Palms Restaurant (Ridgeland)
McCORMICK COUNTY
 Edmunds' and Callie's on Main (McCormick)
 Fannie Kate's (McCormick)

Al's Family Restaurant

Owner or manager:	Al Bone
Address:	611 Atomic Road, North Augusta
Directions:	Atomic Road (SC 125) is the main route between Augusta/North Augusta and the Savannah River Site. Al's is on the tiny stretch of Atomic Road that runs N of US 1. Headed W on US 1 (from Aiken), turn N (right) onto Atomic and continue approx. 2 miles. Restaurant is on left.
Phone number:	803-278-3140
Hours of operation:	MON–SAT 6:00AM–11:00PM
Payment method:	local checks
Reservations:	not needed
Dress:	casual
Gratuity:	not included
Bar:	no
Alcohol:	not served
Diet/light menu:	no
Children's menu:	no
Average price for meal:	$6.50
Discounts:	none offered
Catering:	no
House favorites:	ham hocks, pork chops, fried catfish
Other:	convenient to I-20

If you pull up to a restaurant and the sign out front is advertising a "Bubba Burger," you know the chances are likely you'll find some good country cooking inside. That's the way it is at Al's Family Restaurant in North Augusta.

The restaurant is owned by Al Bone who says he's been in the business nearly all his life. "When I was eleven years old," he recalls, "I was cleaning off tables at a place in Athens, Georgia. Then I was a curb boy at a barbecue restaurant."

When Al finished high school, he joined the army. After his release he moved to North Augusta to work in the security department at what is now the Savannah River Site. "I was there for five years," he said. "Then the Red Pig needed a manager."

In 1963, Al decided he wanted his own place so he bought a bar, Lar Fra, named for the original owners, Larry and Frank. Al immediately converted the bar into a restaurant.

"I had a ground lease there," he said. "I owned the business but leased the land it was on. Then, in 1978, I bought a lot around the corner but found out I couldn't move the name with me. I said, 'That's all right. People know me by now. I'll name the new restaurant after myself.'"

Al says his is a family restaurant. "That doesn't just mean the people who come in here. It is actually a family restaurant. My wife works here; so does my son and daughter-in-law. In fact, they manage the place and my wife's job is to keep me straight." The cook, Ernestine Wright, has worked at the restaurant for thirty years and is just like family. "She's so contrary and ornery," Al teases, "no one else would put up with her. Of course, that shoe fits the other foot, too."

Al's wife, Johnnie, added, "Most of our customers are regulars. In fact, we've got customers I've watched grow up and now they've got children of their own."

Al's breakfast menu includes traditional items like eggs, bacon, and pancakes—and, at least one item that's not so traditional. "I've had truck drivers come in and tell me this is the first restaurant they've been in that serves Spam for breakfast," Al said.

Al's is also one of the few restaurants to serve ham hocks. "They're really delicious. They're really ham shanks but if I called them that, no one would know what they were," the owner says.

For lunch and dinner, there is a regular menu with full meals, sandwiches, and side dishes. However, most people order one of the daily specials ($6.50), which change according to the day of the week. There are usually seven meats to select from and assorted vegetables.

"We have different things on the specials list, but we ordinarily always have pork chops on Tuesdays, Cornish hen on Wednesdays, turkey and dressing on Thursdays, and fried catfish on Fridays. If for some reason we don't have these, customers will ask about them," Johnnie said.

The fried chicken, pork chops, and catfish with catfish stew are offered all-you-can-eat.

Some of Al's other specials include smoked sausage and cabbage, barbecue hash and rice, meat loaf, beef stroganoff with noodles, sirloin tips over rice, beef liver with onion gravy, salmon patties, beef stew, and pot roast.

Examples of sandwiches are hot roast beef ($4), grilled chicken salad ($3.75), fish combo ($3.25), and grilled chicken club ($3.75). The Bubba Burger mentioned on the sign out front (with cooked onions, lettuce, mayonnaise, and mustard) is served with French fries, and tea ($3.25).

♦ North Augusta experienced a population boom in the 1950s with the opening of the Savannah River Plant (known to many older South Carolinians as "the bomb plant").

Country Connection

Owner or manager:	Francis Storey and Jeanette Starnes
Address:	SC 421, Burnettown
Directions:	SC 421 runs parallel to US 1 between Aiken and Augusta, and straight through tiny Burnettown (which is about halfway between the 2 cities). The restaurant is one of the few commercial establishments that make up the town.
Phone number:	803-593-6748
Hours of operation:	MON–FRI 11:00AM–2:00PM
Payment method:	major credit cards
Reservations:	not needed
Dress:	casual
Gratuity:	not included
Bar:	no
Alcohol:	not served
Diet/light menu:	no
Children's menu:	no
Average price for meal:	$5.00
Discounts:	none offered
Catering:	no
House favorites:	potato soup, broccoli salad
Other:	convenient to I-20

Frances Storey and Jeanette Starnes have been friends all their lives. But since the opening of their restaurant, the Country Connection, that friendship has been strained at times.

"There have been times when I could just kill her," Frances admitted. "Of course, I'm sure there have been times when she felt like that about me." Frances recalls her friend assuring her that having their own business would be fun. "I keep asking her when the fun begins," she joked.

The idea of opening a restaurant started with Jeanette's handmade crafts. She wanted a place where she could sell them and suggested a restaurant-gift shop. There were two problems with the idea. One was that Frances already had a job. The second was that neither woman knew a thing about running a restaurant.

The first problem was easily overcome. Frances quit her job. The second was a bit more difficult.

"We had no idea what we were doing," Jeanette says. "We rode around half an hour just trying to find the place to get a sales tax license. We didn't know what companies sold food nor what was available."

The first step, they decided, was to find a location. The women had noticed a little blue house on SC Hwy. 421 in Burnettown. It appeared to be empty so they tracked down the owner and made arrangements to rent it. The house had four rooms in front, a kitchen, and a storeroom. The entrepreneurs decided that two of the rooms would serve as the dining rooms and the other two could be the gift shop.

The two friends originally planned to sell cakes in the establishment. One Christmas season they made over 100 cakes; customers were still picking them up at midnight before Christmas Eve. "Frances finally said, 'I can't take it any more! I'm going to tie a red ribbon around this building and give it as a Christmas present to the next person who comes in,'" Jeanette said, laughing. The cake business was eliminated and the crafts business reduced to just one room.

When Country Connection first opened, the restaurant averaged only ten customers a day. The menu was fairly simple, consisting of a few sandwiches, a couple of salads, and a soup.

After its modest beginning, the business began to grow. Word of the two women and their good food spread. With the influx of new customers, the menu was expanded to half a dozen meals in addition to a complete selection of sandwiches, salads, soups, and one dessert per day.

The potato soup is a real treat ($1.50). This delectable dish has bits of ham and cheese sprinkled over the top. Corned beef on a croissant (with side dish, $4.50) is just one of the delicious sandwiches offered. More complete meals (around $4.95) include liver and onions, ham steak, fried chicken, and grilled chicken breast with ham and cheese.

Country Connection opens at 11:00 AM but the two women get in at 8:00 because they make their own salad dressings, soups, and desserts. Despite the fact that Frances jokes about not having any fun yet, she admits that the project has been a success. "I think the reason it works is that we are so different. Jeanette isn't interested in ordering supplies or handling the money. She concentrates on running the restaurant. What worries me doesn't bother her and vice versa. So we get along pretty well."

♦ The city of Aiken is home to the Thoroughbred Hall of Fame. Many famous race horses have been trained in the area.

Variety Restaurant

Owner or manager:	Jimmy Varos
Address:	921 York Street (US 1), Aiken
Directions:	US 1 runs through the town of Aiken, becoming York Street inside city limits. Entering Aiken on US 1 from NE, go through 2nd stop light (Rutland Avenue), then 1/4 mile to restaurant.
Phone number:	803-648-6987
Hours of operation:	MON–SAT 5:00–10:30PM
Payment method:	major credit cards
Reservations:	not accepted
Dress:	casual
Gratuity:	not included
Bar:	yes
Alcohol:	yes
Diet/light menu:	no
Children's menu:	yes
Average price for meal:	$15.00
Discounts:	none offered
Catering:	no
House favorites:	steaks, seafood, hamburgers, specials offered
Other:	convenient to I-20

If ever there was a restaurant that does not splurge on the exterior of its building, it is Variety Restaurant in Aiken. The casual observer driving by the building would probably think it had closed down years earlier. But the Variety's customers don't go there for the looks, they go for the good food.

If you go into the Variety very often, you'll soon start recognizing the other patrons. "About eighty percent of our customers are regulars," owner Jimmy Varos explains. "Some come in several times a week, others once a week or maybe twice a month."

The restaurant may be the only one in town that has been

around longer than the famous Savannah River Site. The "bomb plant" is forty-five years old. The Variety is fifty-five. Jimmy, whose family is Greek, has owned the restaurant for over fourteen years. His background lends itself well to his business.

Jimmy left home when he was only fourteen, and after a few years on his own enlisted with the Merchant Marines. They taught him how to cook and he served in that capacity for over eight years. After being discharged, he ran a fish market and gained expertise in seafood. Both of these earlier experiences gave Jimmy the proper background for taking over the Variety. He is assisted in the operation of the place by his girlfriend, Susan Ekonomakis.

The dirt parking lot starts to fill up quite early, especially on Friday and Saturday nights. Someone once said that a restaurant in the South could be judged by the number of pickup trucks and Cadillacs parked out front. By this standard, the Variety would earn five stars.

Susan explains the draw. "The Variety is known for steaks and large portions. We have been voted as having the best steaks in Aiken County. Our biggest cut is a thirty-two-ounce steak. I've seen people eat it, though I don't know how they do it."

The menu is fairly extensive, offering among other things hamburgers, seafood, chicken, and spaghetti. No matter what you order you will agree that everything is served in large—some might say gigantic—portions. The size of the hamburgers makes you wonder if the obliging cows were raised on the grounds of the nearby nuclear plant.

With Jimmy's background in seafood, it is no wonder that item is one of their specialties. He personally selects all seafood that is served. In addition, he makes his own breading and tartar sauce, mixes his own seasoning, and prepares everything to order. The jumbo fried shrimp ($14.95), king seafood platter ($16.95), fried catfish ($13.85), and snow crabs ($22.95) are just some of the favorites from the sea.

Most of the steaks, such as the sixteen-ounce ribeye ($14.85) and the sixteen-ounce New York strip ($18.85) are cut by Jimmy in the kitchen.

The owner has a kitchen staff that has been with him for years, so he can now spend more time visiting with his customers in the dining room. Susan says this allows all his customers to meet him. "They want to talk with him and shake his hand so he's had to turn over some of the cooking to others."

While some of the prices might appear a bit high, you will not come away from the Variety feeling cheated. If you are hungry for good food and lots of it, this is definitely a place for you.

Village Inn

Owner or manager:	Cliff Rogers
Address:	US 301 N, Allendale
Directions:	From Allendale, follow US 301 N. The restaurant is just outside town on the left. There is a large sign.
Phone number:	803-584-4674
Hours of operation:	SUN–FRI 11:00AM–2:00PM
Payment method:	checks
Reservations:	required only for Christmas buffet
Dress:	casual
Gratuity:	not included
Bar:	no
Alcohol:	not served
Diet/light menu:	no
Children's menu:	child's plate available
Average price for meal:	$6.00, weekday • $7.50, Sunday
Discounts:	none offered
Catering:	yes—extensive
House favorites:	fried chicken, fresh vegetables

Cliff Rodgers, the owner of Village Inn in Allendale, is quick to point out that his main business is catering. However, his restaurant is open from 11:00 AM to 2:00 PM Sunday through Friday so the local folks don't miss out on the good cuisine.

"You've heard of the movie *Never on Sunday*? Well, we're *never* [open] *on Saturday* because that is our busiest catering day," he said.

He considers the work he does at the restaurant and the catering two different businesses. The big thing at Village Inn is the buffet, though you can order items off the menu every day but Sunday. Unlike some buffets, Cliff goes to great measure for all his food.

"We fix a cucumber salad that no one else has the recipe for. We have a squash casserole that's fantastic. It's got cream

cheese and walnuts in it. Our sweet potato souffle is made
from real sweet potatoes cooked that morning. We always have
creamed corn cut off the cob. We do a potato casserole that has
sour cream, a couple different cheeses, and mushrooms. And
don't forget the fried chicken. In other words, it is very southern food," he said.

The buffet has just about everything you could imagine.
An even bigger spread is laid, however, the Sunday before
Christmas. "It's all the special traditional holiday dishes. You
have to have reservations and, even so, the line goes out the
door and encircles the building," Cliff says.

The restaurant's food is definitely traditional. Many are
surprised to find that the catering end of the business has a
different slant. It has to be, since ninety-five percent of the catering jobs are formal occasions.

"I have a whole room piled high with crystal, silver, china,
linens, candelabra, and over 250 baskets. In fact, the room got
so full I had to add a room onto my house for the overflow,"
the owner said.

Some of his catering accessories are quite unique. He has
an eighteenth-century artillery basket that he piles high with
fruit. There are birdhouses modeled after historic churches in
Beaufort County. In front of these he places candles, which
look like street lights leading up to each church. He uses
hunter green tablecloths with white French china.

"The catering business is not confined geographically. I've
done parties in Georgia as far south as the Florida line. I've
done Jekyll Island and all the beaches. I've gone to Aiken,
Orangeburg, Savannah, and Charleston. I've done catering for
The Citadel but if I could cater something at Clemson, I'd
think I had died and gone to heaven," confesses Cliff, a former
Clemson student and lifelong Tiger fan.

Until Clemson comes calling, Cliff has more than enough
work to keep him busy. Recently he did a prime rib dinner for
420. That same day he did an hors d'oeuvres party—and when
Cliff says "hors d'oeuvres," he means serious eating. He served

marinated quail, oysters on the half shell, two kinds of cheese ball, and all kinds of cheese, spreads, and delicacies.

"We have a fruit dip of white chocolate and almonds that will make you want to call the preacher," he exclaimed. "It's that sinful."

Cliff had not planned to get into the food business. He started out helping William Mixon, who originally opened Village Inn, with a catering job. When the owner decided to sell the restaurant, Cliff jumped in.

Whether it is country cooking in the restaurant or fine dining at a catered function, you will not be disappointed by Village Inn.

♦ South Carolina's state dog is the Boykin Spaniel.

Denmark Diner

Owner or manager:	Robert Funderburk
Address:	123 W. Baruch Street, Denmark
Directions:	US 321 and US 78 intersect in town of Denmark. From W (Aiken/Blackville), follow US 78 into town. Just past RR tracks, restaurant is on the right. (At end of this block, US 78 and US 321 meet.)
Phone number:	803-793-0400
Hours of operation:	TUE–THU 11:30AM–2:00PM; FRI 11:30AM–2:00PM, 6:00–9:00PM; SAT 6:00–9:00PM; SUN 12:00N–3:00PM
Payment method:	major credit cards
Reservations:	not needed
Dress:	casual
Gratuity:	not included
Bar:	none
Alcohol:	not served
Diet/light menu:	baked entrees without sauce or gravy
Children's menu:	none
Average price for meal:	$5.00, lunch • $11.00, dinner
Discounts:	none
Catering:	weddings, private parties
House favorites:	shrimp and grits, red snapper

Sometimes you go into a restaurant and see pictures of show business or sports personalities on the walls. Not so at Denmark Diner. The pictures there are of political figures. That's because owner Robert Funderburk was associated with various restaurants in the nation's capital and some of the best eating establishments in South Carolina's capital city. (The largest photo in the diner is of Robert with Gerald Ford, taken when Robert was in charge of Ford's vice presidential inaugural banquet.)

"I'm from Lancaster and I used to go north in the summers to work," Robert said. "I met the food and beverage manager of Marriott Corporation, and when I graduated, he hired me." After five years with Marriott, Robert went to work for the Sheraton Hotel where he served in various capacities: storeroom steward, banquet steward, and kitchen steward.

After returning to South Carolina in 1974, Robert worked at the Summit Club in Columbia for seven years and then served as general manager of the Capital City Club. While in Columbia, he formed an acquaintance with Dr. James Holderman, president of the University of South Carolina at the time, and was offered the position of general manager of USC's Faculty House.

When Robert decided it was time to get away from the hustle and bustle, he and his wife moved to Denmark, his wife's hometown, and opened up the diner. Though Robert is no longer feeding the high-brow political crowd, his goal of providing quality food and service has not diminished.

Visitors will be taken aback when they first enter Denmark Diner. Waitress Lea Anne Ferrell said many first-time customers are surprised to find linen tableclothes and proper dinner service for evening meals. "Eventually I'd like to get into tableside cooking," Robert said, "things like steak Diane, crepes, and bananas foster."

The food and atmosphere of Denmark Diner are both excellent. A favorite item on the menu is sauteed shrimp and grits (a dish of grits surrounded by sauteed shrimp, onions, and mushrooms, served with a demiglace, $10). You might also check out the chicken a la maison (boneless breast of chicken sauteed with shrimp and served with white wine sauce, $11.95).

The lunchtime menu is not elaborate but nevertheless tasty. It includes chicken salad ($6.50), sauteed chicken breast (with marinated vegetables and fruit, $5), and barbecue open-face sandwich (with potato salad and coleslaw, $5.50).

When you're in the mood to enjoy upscale dining in a quiet, relaxed atmosphere (while discussing politics), Denmark Diner is the ideal place to go.

Miller's
Bread-Basket

Owner or manager:	Ray Miller
Address:	Main Street, Blackville
Directions:	From Aiken (W), take US 78 into Blackville. Turn left onto SC 3. Continue one block, then turn right onto Main Street. Restaurant is on right, in first block.
Phone number:	803-284-3117
Hours of operation:	MON–SAT 11:00AM–2:00PM
	TUE, THU, FRI 5:00–8:00PM
Payment method:	major credit cards
Reservations:	not needed
Dress:	casual
Gratuity:	not included
Bar:	no
Alcohol:	not served
Diet/light menu:	no
Children's menu:	no
Average price for meal:	$5.95, one trip • $6.95, all-you-can-eat
Discounts:	none offered
Catering:	no
House favorites:	homemade bread and desserts
Other:	gift shop

Ray Miller, owner of Miller's Bread-Basket in Blackville, poses a question that has probably crossed many traveler's minds. "Did you ever notice that wherever there is a Mennonite or Amish community, there is always a good restaurant?"

Ray explains the phenomenon this way: "Most of our women do not work outside the home when the children are young. Therefore, they perfect their homemaking skills, things like sewing and cooking."

That's been the way of life for this religious sect for generations. As the children get older, many women begin to have available time to use their cooking skills outside the home.

"When we first came to Blackville," Ray said, "I worked

at a couple of things, like being in a paint and body shop. But my wife and I had always had a hankering to have a restaurant."

This "hankering" was repressed until the Miller children were older. When two of them had married and moved away and the others were big enough to work, Miller's Bread-Basket was opened. That was twelve years ago.

"Susie's in charge of the cooking and I'm the PR guy," Ray says. Ray is in constant motion in the restaurant, moving from table to table visiting with customers, all the while keeping an eye on the work the waitresses are doing. He also has another duty. "I'm the chief taster," he says, laughing.

But don't believe for a second that Ray's only skills are public relations and tasting food. Actually his most important skill is baking bread, one of the big drawing cards for the restaurant—as you might have guessed by the restaurant's name. He arrives each morning at 4:00 AM and spends the next several hours baking loaf after loaf. He makes on average eighty to ninety loaves a day. Even with this huge number, it is not uncommon for the restaurant to sell out during the day. About half the day's baking is sold sliced with meals. The other half is purchased by the loaf by customers to take home with them. Bread lovers from throughout the area flock to enjoy Ray's specialty.

"I make five or six different kinds each day. It depends on what ingredients I have. Like the butternut bread takes four flavorings, three sweeteners, nuts, and coconut. In all, there's fifteen or sixteen ingredients," he says.

The bread, which runs from $1.25 to $2.25 a loaf, is available in garlic, onion, butternut, cheese, honey oat, cinnamon raisin, white, wheat, apple cinnamon, and banana nut.

But don't think for a minute the bread is the only draw to the place. Miller's Bread-Basket has another claim to fame: its pies. They are made right in the restaurant and include coconut cream, German chocolate, pecan, sweet potato custard, strawberry, lemon meringue, and shoofly.

"It's funny about shoofly pie. In the North we've always eaten the pie but never knew the song. Southerners know the song but usually have never had the pie. I'm from Indiana; we eat the pie but not like the people in Pennsylvania. They'll eat it for breakfast, lunch, and dinner," explains Ray.

Meals are served buffet style. The food is very traditional and includes a large selection of meats and vegetables. Everything is made from scratch. Whether it is lunch or dinner, your stomach will definitely be full when your plate is empty.

After a meal at Miller's Bread-Basket, you'll be left with only one question: when will I be able to come back?

♦ Barnwell County is home to Healing Springs. The community boasts several artesian wells whose water is believed to have healing power. People travel from miles around to collect this water for home use.

Winton Inn

Owner or manager:	Charles Webb
Address:	1003 Marlboro Ave., Barnwell
Directions:	Entering Barnwell town limit on SC 3 (Marlboro Avenue) from Blackville, continue S through town approx. 3 miles to US 278 (Jackson Street). Restaurant located on southern end of town where SC 3 and US 278 converge.
Phone number:	803-259-7181
Hours of operation:	MON–SAT 6:00AM–10:00PM
Payment method:	major credit cards
Reservations:	recommended for groups of 8 or more
Dress:	casual to dressy
Gratuity:	not included
Bar:	no
Alcohol:	beer and wine
Diet/light menu:	salads
Children's menu:	yes
Average price for meal:	$4.00, breakfast • $3.50, lunch • $12.00, dinner
Discounts:	none offered
Catering:	no
House favorites:	prime rib/seafood buffet (THU–SAT 6:00–10:00PM)
Other:	take-out available

The casual visitor might think the Winton Inn in Barnwell is owned by the Winton family. But a student of South Carolina history would understand the name.

During and following the Revolutionary War, the state was separated into districts. This particular area of the state was named Winton District in 1785 to honor Gen. Richard Winn, a popular political figure for whom the town of Winnsboro is also named.

The district kept this name for only fourteen years, however. In 1798 it was changed to Barnwell to honor Winn's rival,

General Barnwell. It is interesting to note that the State Senate Journal continued to call the district Winton until 1810.

Considering its brief use, it is no surprise the name Winton has been forgotten by most South Carolinians. It is still memorialized, however, by the Winton Inn, opened in 1979 by Charles Webb, who changed the name to reflect the area's history.

"Before that, it had been a much smaller restaurant called The Sherwood," Mary Jo Delk explains. "In fact, this building has been a restaurant for over forty years." Mary Jo has been with Charles Webb since he first opened Winton Inn and now manages the business for him. "Originally there were three owners, but Mr. Webb is the only one left," she said.

Changes were made to the old place when Winton Inn opened. First, the building was enlarged. The original section now serves as the kitchen. The new dining room was freshly decorated in southern decor, as you would expect. The forest green walls are adorned with hand painted magnolia blossoms.

Open for business for twenty years, Winton Inn has established a faithful customer base. One visit will make the reasons obvious. The place is reknown for its salad bar. Piled high with fruits, vegetables, and cheeses, the bar dominates the dining room. It is billed on the menu as "one of the Southeast's finest salad bars."

Equally impressive is the dinner buffet table, featuring prime rib, crab legs, Carolina Bog, shrimp, and a selection of seafood. Priced at $16.95, it is an all-you-can-eat extravaganza. "Of course all the locals know about our buffet, but we also get people traveling here from Savannah, Augusta, and other places," Mary Jo said.

Not everyone is going to be hungry enough to tackle such a mountain of food. People falling in this category can choose from the twelve-ounce New York strip ($12.95), the eight-ounce filet mignon ($13.95), the seafood platter ($13.95), fried oysters ($9.95), Italian grilled chicken ($8.95), or chicken breast teriyaki ($9.95).

For lunch you can select from a number of sandwiches: steak and cheese ($5.95), hot roast beef ($4.50), fried ham ($2.25), or hamburger ($2.50). Soups, such as catfish stew and clam chowder, are popular choices for lighter eaters.

♦ Tourism is among South Carolina's top industries.

Old McDonald Fish Camp

Owner or manager:	Jerry and Jackie Bass
Address:	355 Currytown Road, North Augusta
Directions:	From I-20 (N. Augusta), take US 25 (exit 5) N 1.4 miles. Turn left onto Sweetwater Road, go 1 mile. Turn left on Currytown Road, go approx. 1.2 miles. Restaurant is on left (just inside Edgefield County, at Aiken County line). Few hwy. signs; many fish camp signs.
Phone number:	803-279-3305
Hours of operation:	THU 5:00–9:00PM, FRI–SAT 5:00–9:30PM
Payment method:	major credit cards
Reservations:	not needed
Dress:	casual
Gratuity:	not included
Bar:	no
Alcohol:	not served
Diet/light menu:	no
Children's menu:	yes
Average price for meal:	$12.00
Discounts:	seniors
Catering:	hosts private parties of 50 or more—weekdays only
House favorites:	catfish
Other:	great place for kids

If you're going to open a restaurant and your last name is Bass, it would make sense that your place specialize in seafood. At least that's what Jerry Bass figured twenty years ago when he opened Old McDonald Fish Camp. And, there weren't many seafood places around at the time.

The decision for Jerry to enter the food business came easy. During Jerry's childhood, his father opened and operated three Howard Johnson's. Once he reached the ninth grade, Jerry began working in the restaurants. "When you're raised in the restaurant business, it gets into your blood," he said.

The catchy name of his establishment originated through the familiar nursery rhyme about the farmer with the name McDonald. Jerry and his wife, Jackie, thought it would be fun to have a few animals around their place. The menagerie has grown as the restaurant has. What started out as a building with seating for 95 has been expanded to now hold 250. With the increase of seats came an increase in animals. This collection now includes Texas longhorn cattle, pygmy goats, peacocks, ducks, geese, chickens, and a potbellied pig. "The kids love to come here to feed the animals. And wherever the kids want to go is where you're probably going to go," Jerry reasoned.

When the restaurant first opened, it stood beside a four-acre pond. That pond has now been extended to surround the building and a moat has been dug across the front, making the lot on which the building sits a virtual island. Visitors walk across the moat on a covered bridge to reach the front porch. If you have to wait on the porch to be seated, you can watch the large schools of fish swim in the pond.

Jerry oversees the business and Jackie acts as hostess. Their son is in charge of the kitchen and the couple's two sons-in-law help cook. Their two daughters and a daughter-in-law work as waitresses.

Each meal is begun with complimentary hushpuppies and grits. As the restaurant's name implies, the house specialty is seafood—prepared fried or broiled, customer's preference.

"Twenty years ago we fried everything," Jerry said, "but people have become much more health conscious. And back then, we hadn't even heard of baked potatoes. Now, about seventy percent of our customers order them over french fries."

The most popular item on the menu is catfish (all you can eat, $11.50—$1 off on Thursday). For the same price, those who prefer may choose fish fillet or perch (also all you can eat). Other popular choices include broiled shrimp (large, $11.25; small, $9.75), fried or broiled sea scallops ($12.25), broiled fish fillet stuffed with crabmeat ($12.50), and frog legs ($11.50). Any of these items will satisfy the hungriest of appetites.

With over two decades in business, Jerry Bass is certainly doing something right. And even though you can order a hamburger from the menu, you will definitely not confuse this restaurant with another that has a similar name.

Ten Governors Cafe

Owner or manager:	Glenn Hammond
Address:	109 Court House Square, Edgefield
Directions:	From I-20, take SC 19 (exit 18) NW approx. 10 miles to US 25. Continue NW on US 25 about 5 miles; take US 25BUS 1 mile to town square, downtown. Restaurant is on left side of square, facing courthouse.
Phone number:	803-637-9050
Hours of operation:	MON–SAT 8:00AM–9:00PM
Payment method:	major credit cards
Reservations:	not needed
Dress:	casual
Gratuity:	not included
Bar:	no
Alcohol:	not served
Diet/light menu:	salads, vegetable plate
Children's menu:	no
Average price for meal:	$3.00, breakfast • $4.50, lunch • $4.50, dinner
Discounts:	none
Catering:	yes
House favorites:	chef's salad with chicken, chicken tenders, hamburger steaks

When Glenn Hammond decided to open a restaurant, Ten Governors Cafe seemed a logical choice for a name. Edgefield is home to ten South Carolina governors—in fact, one of them, James Hammond who served between 1842 and 1844, is an ancestor of Glenn. Besides, "Welcome to Historic Edgefield, Home of Ten Governors" was printed on the side of the old brick building where Glenn was planning to locate his restaurant.

"The building was a department store for years, back to the 1940s," Glenn said. "Then for a short time it was a chiropractor's office." Of course, there were a lot of renovations needed to change the store–office space into a restaurant.

Glenn took care of these renovations himself, working for three months to get everything ready. "I knew how to do them because I had been in the construction business for fifteen years," he said, adding that he had changed careers to "get out of the sun."

"I've been cooking since I was five years old. My mother was sick quite a bit so I had to learn." Glenn's wife, Amey, added that her father-in-law was also a cook, widely known for his barbeque and fish stew.

Ten Governors Cafe opened October 25, 1997, and has been a popular eatery in Edgefield ever since. Regular customers come in several times a week because the menu changes daily. "They know exactly what they want when they come in," Glenn says.

Besides the local folks, you never know who you might see at Ten Governors. Glenn showed off some pictures of his more famous clientele. Looking at one of Sen. Strom Thurmond, he said, "He comes in every time he's in town. In fact, he was here just two weeks ago."

Other politicians have visited the place and Glenn has photos of U.S. Rep. Lindsay Graham and S.C. Rep. Bill Clyburn to prove it.

The restaurant is open from 8:00 AM to 9:00 PM, Monday through Saturday. "I'm here most of the time. Last Saturday I worked fifteen hours but usually I put in about twelve hours a day," he said.

Homecooked meals include one meat, three vegetables, and bread ($5.25) or one meat, two vegetables, and bread ($4.75). Daily offerings change. On Monday, there might be fried chicken, fried shrimp, and roast beef; on Tuesday, turkey, baked chicken, and cube steak. Vegetables might include butter peas, coleslaw, macaroni and cheese, asparagus casserole, and squash.

Sandwiches such as hamburger ($3.25), hot dog ($2.25), club ($4.50), and grilled chicken breast ($3.50) are available as well as salads: chicken salad ($4.00), chef's salad with ham or chicken ($3.50), and regular salad ($1.50)

Desserts are $1.25. Some are homemade; others are bought.

Breakfast is served from 8:00 to 10:30 AM. Offerings include one egg, choice of ham or bacon or sausage, grits, and biscuit ($3.00); the same meal with two eggs ($3.75); and bacon, ham, or sausage biscuit ($1.00).

Blazers
Restaurant

Owner or manager:	Jimmy and Norma Britt
Address:	US 72, Greenwood
Directions:	From Greenwood, take US 221/SC 72 N, toward Lake Greenwood (Laurens County line), approx. 7 miles. Restaurant is on right, just before lake.
Phone number:	864-223-1917
Hours of operation:	TUE–SAT 5:00–10:00PM
Payment method:	checks, major credit cards
Reservations:	not accepted
Dress:	casual
Gratuity:	15% on groups of 8 or more
Bar:	yes
Alcohol:	yes
Diet/light menu:	limited choices
Children's menu:	yes ($3.99)
Average price for meal:	$10.00
Discounts:	none offered
Catering:	no
House favorites:	shrimp and grits, filet mignon, seafood platter
Other:	complimentary shrimp dip for all tables

When a couple keeps a restaurant running successfully for over twenty years, you know they're doing something right. That's the case with Jimmy and Norma Britt, owners of Blazers Restaurant since 1976.

Prior to entering the restaurant business, the couple owned a construction company. In 1973 they acquired the property on Lake Greenwood where Blazers is located. After leasing the property to someone who unsuccessfully ran a restaurant there for three years, the Britts took it over and soon closed their construction business.

Over the years, the restaurant has become a family affair. All five of the Britts' children and some of their grandchildren have been employed at the restaurant. Jimmy is the most visible Britt. He makes a point of stopping at each table to speak with customers.

Jimmy is an advocate of independent restaurant owners. He served as director of the National Restaurant Association (the first from South Carolina) and is currently an honorary national director, a distinction given only to those who serve at least nine years as director. (He proudly points out that Dave Thomas of Wendy's fame has been a director but did not serve long enough to become an honorary member.) Jimmy has also served as president of the S.C. Restaurant Association.

Norma and Jimmy pride themselves on the fact that all entrees are cooked after the order is placed. This allows customers to have food prepared the way they wish. Seafood favorites include the seafood platter ($13.99), shrimp ($10.99), yellow fin tuna ($14.99), shrimp jambalaya ($9.99), and the ever-popular shrimp and grits ($9.99). If you're a pasta fan, there is seafood and angel hair pasta ($12.99) and chicken/broccoli fettucine alfredo ($12.99). If you don't eat seafood, there are plenty of other choices: baby back ribs (half, $7.99; full, $13.99), quail and frog legs ($9.99), and a variety of steaks. Norma says the filet mignon ($14.99) is her personal favorite.

Each table is given an appetizer of shrimp dip to enjoy prior to the meal. The dip, available in regular or hot and made in-house, has become so popular, it is now available for purchase in grocery stores throughout the Carolinas and Georgia.

Before leaving the restaurant, be sure to fill out a special occasion card. You will receive a $5 coupon on your birthday and wedding anniversary each year to use on your next visit.

Customers drive from Laurens, Newberry, Greenville, and Spartanburg Counties to eat at Blazers. Those traveling by boat on Lake Greenwood may "park" at one of the three available docks. If you're not hungry but just want a cocktail, the entire upstairs is a bar. From there, you can enjoy a great view of the lake.

The next time you want good seafood but can't get to the beach, visit Blazers. It's sure to satisfy your taste buds.

Rick's Uptown Cafeteria

Owner or manager:	Richard Sheppard
Address:	234 Pressley Street, Greenwood
Directions:	US 25 runs through Greenwood, becoming Main Street downtown. Follow Main to Pressley Street. Turn onto Pressley, between Nations Bank and Greenwood County Bank. Restaurant is on left, at end of first block.
Phone number:	864-223-6545
Hours of operation:	MON–SAT 5:30AM–4:00PM SUN 11:00AM–4:00PM
Payment method:	cash only
Reservations:	not needed
Dress:	casual
Gratuity:	not included
Bar:	no
Alcohol:	not served
Diet/light menu:	no
Children's menu:	yes
Average price for meal:	$4.95
Discounts:	none offered
Catering:	yes
House favorites:	fried chicken, collards
Other:	banquet room available

After working in the restaurant business for ten years, Rick Sheppard knew he wanted to open up his own place in Greenwood. He had only one thing to consider: what kind of restaurant should it be.

"Greenwood has a good many sandwich shops and fast food places," Rick explains. "I thought what the town needed was a place where folks could get good country cooking. I decided I'd serve the food I liked to eat."

Rick got into the business soon after college when he went to work for McDonald's. During his decade with the hamburger giant, he learned two important things: who the food vendors were and how a successful restaurant operates.

Obviously the education received at McDonald's paid off. Rick's has prospered since it first opened on Main Street in downtown Greenwood. Realizing he could use all the advice he could get, he hired cooks who contributed ideas to the menu. He also incorporated recipes from his mother and grandmother. The restaurant even came up with a slogan: "Best Home Cooked Food in Town."

As his customer base grew, Rick needed more space. In 1995 he built a new place on Pressley Street about a block behind his old building. He soon found that even his new facility wasn't big enough. "Before the year was over, I had built onto the new building, enlarging the kitchen and adding a banquet room," the owner says.

Rick's opens at 5:30 AM and serves a traditional southern breakfast. The remainder of the day food is served buffet style (one meat, three vegetables, and a drink, $4.95; one meat, two vegetables, and a drink, $4.75; vegetable plate and drink, $4.50). The buffet features four meats, such as fried chicken, meat loaf, pork chops, and liver. Vegetables are family favorites: black-eyed peas, green beans, collards, creamed corn, steamed cabbage, broccoli and cheese, and various casseroles.

"We have some customers that come in every single day. Some of them work downtown; others come from elsewhere. I vary the menu so they can have something different to choose from each day," Rick says.

Rick has learned that operating and managing his own restaurant is hard work. He arrives well before the 5:30 AM opening. And the 4:00 PM closing time is the signal to begin preparing for the next day. Add to this a successful catering business—private parties, wedding receptions, and business meetings.

McDonald's may claim to have served "billions worldwide," but Rick is happy to simply serve the citizens of Greenwood. From the looks of it, he's doing a good job.

Ernie's Restaurant

Owner or manager:	Brenda Kinsey
Address:	722 Elm Street, Hampton
Directions:	US 278 becomes Elm Street in downtown Hampton. Headed SE on US 278 continue through downtown till you come to Hardees; go 2 blocks. Ernies is on left.
Phone number:	803-943-3002
Hours of operation:	MON–SAT 6:00AM–10:00PM
	SUN 8:00AM–9:00PM
Payment method:	major credit cards
Reservations:	required for private dining room only
Dress:	casual
Gratuity:	not included
Bar:	no
Alcohol:	not served
Diet/light menu:	chicken, tuna, and shrimp salad; salad bar
Children's menu:	children under 3 eat free
Average price for meal:	buffet, $5.75 • meal, $7.00
Discounts:	10% to seniors
Catering:	yes
House favorites:	buffet, hamburger steak
Other:	private dining room available for large parties

Brenda Kinsey has done it all at Ernie's Restaurant in Hampton. She began her employment as a dishwasher. Then she became a waitress, next a cook, and eventually an office worker. When her family stepped in to purchase the business, Brenda made it all the way to the top.

"About seven years ago, my parents took over the place and I became manager," Brenda said.

Brenda's parents, John and Mary Ann Standley, own two restaurants that bear the name Ernie's. One is in Hampton, the other in nearby Estill.

"I take care of the Hampton one and they are back and

forth between the two," Brenda explains.

Ernie's can best be described as a country restaurant. The food is homecooked, and the decor is rustic. The parking lot is always full, especially during weekday lunch hour when many local workers converge to enjoy a great, inexpensive meal.

"I moved to Hampton four years ago from Ehrhardt. Brenda said. "By now, I know just about everybody in town."

Brenda really enjoys her job, despite the long hours that are often required. Ernie's is open from 6:00 AM to 10:00 PM every day except Sunday when the hours are 8:00 AM to 9:00 PM. "I'm in and out all day long," she said. "And we divide up the day among several crews. Fortunately, they're all very good. The majority of our people were here when I first came seven years ago."

Ernie's features a buffet that includes a hot bar, a salad bar, and iced tea or coffee ($5.75). Additionally, you can order from the menu, items such as half a fried chicken ($6.95), pork chops ($7.95), and fried shrimp ($9.00).

The breakfast menu is traditional southern fare: bacon, eggs, sausage, pancakes, biscuits, and other favorites.

The in-house dining is just part of Ernie's business. "We do a lot of catering. We fix food for churches, homecomings, funerals, and private parties—any occasion at all," Brenda said.

Though locals make up the bulk of its customer base, the restaurant benefits from the many visitors routinely passing through Hampton. Ernie's is on US Hwy. 278, which crosses the Georgia border at Augusta and runs to Hilton Head Island. It's a convenient stop for those heading to the coast. US Hwy. 601, a North to South route, which many take to Savannah, runs through Hampton near Ernie's, making it a suitable place for a meal break for those travelers as well.

Ernie's is the type of restaurant for families who once enjoyed dining at the old-fashioned truck stops, where they could get good food at reasonable prices. While it is hard to find this sort of truck stop nowadays, folks passing through Hampton are fortunate to have an alternative: Ernie's.

Palms Restaurant

Owner or manager:	Esther Cooler
Address:	US 17 S, Ridgeland
Directions:	US 17 runs through small town of Ridgeland. Restaurant is downtown, on W side of street, beside Palms Inn. (I-95 runs parallel to US 17, about 1 mile away.)
Phone number:	843-726-5509
Hours of operation:	MON–SAT 7:00AM–10:00PM SUN 7:00AM–3:00PM
Payment method:	major credit cards
Reservations:	recommended on Sunday
Dress:	casual
Gratuity:	included for large groups
Bar:	no
Alcohol:	beer and wine
Diet/light menu:	cold plate, boiled shrimp, salads
Children's menu:	no
Average price for meal:	$4.00, breakfast • $5.00, lunch • $10.00, dinner
Discounts:	none offered
Catering:	yes
House favorites:	fried shrimp
Other:	Their shrimp was featured in *Gourmet Magazine*.

Experts will tell you it is a good idea to be familiar with a type of business before you think about buying. When Esther Cooler decided to buy Palms Restaurant in 1983, she didn't have to do any research into the establishment or that particular area of business. Having been a waitress there for over twenty-five years, she knew everything there was to know.

Esther had first come to the restaurant in 1956 as a way to supplement her living. "In the early years I had two jobs. I was the housekeeper on one of the plantations around here. When the house was closed up after the winter, I always came right back to the restaurant," she explained.

Eventually, Esther gave up her housekeeping job and went to work at the Jasper County dining establishment full-time. She started as a waitress but soon took on additional duties. She got to know the business so well she began handling all orders and eventually took over management of the day-to-day operations. When the owner decided to retire, it seemed only natural that Esther purchase Palms.

Located in the heart of the small town of Ridgeland, much of the restaurant's business comes from tourists and Low Country residents outside the immediate area. "Our clientele is a lot of local folks," Esther says. "By local I mean Hilton Head, Savannah, and Bluffton. We have some customers that have been coming for years on their way home from vacation."

One of the big draws to the restaurant is the dessert selection. Esther said her biggest job at Palms is that of pie baker. Each day she makes a variety of pies, including chocolate, coconut, and lemon. "People come in and buy whole pies," she stated. "Of course, they have to let us know ahead of time."

Pies alone are not the only draw. People flock to Palms each Sunday for the big buffet. The all-you-can-eat feast contains something for everyone—for only $9.00. A slightly scaled down version of the buffet is offered during the week for $6.00.

In addition to the buffet, for lunch Esther offers various salads (such as chicken salad, $3.00), and sandwiches (such as barbecue, $2.25; steak, $4.95; and hamburger, $2.50). For the evening meal, choices include such items as ribeye steak ($11.95), chopped sirloin with mushroom gravy ($7.25), and southern fried chicken (half, $7.50; quarter, $6.50).

With its proximity to the coast, it is no surprise there are a number of seafood dishes (such as filet of flounder, broiled or fried, $7.25; and lobster tails, $14.95). If you enjoy shrimp, Palms is definitely the place for you. Their recipe was featured in *Gourmet* Magazine and is Esther's personal favorite.

Customers of Palms Restaurant know they are guaranteed two things: good food and an owner who knows her business.

Edmunds' and Callie's on Main

Owner or manager:	Callie Patterson
Address:	222 S. Main Street, McCormick
Directions:	US 378 and SC 28 intersect downtown McCormick. Restaurant is at this intersection, facing SC 28 (Main Street).
Phone number:	864-465-3225
Hours of operation:	MON–WED 7:00AM–2:00PM; THU–SAT 7:00AM–2:00PM, 5:00–9:00PM; SUN 11:00AM–2:00PM
Payment method:	major credit cards
Reservations:	not needed
Dress:	casual
Gratuity:	not included
Bar:	no
Alcohol:	not served
Diet/light menu:	salads, broiled dishes
Children's menu:	yes
Average price for meal:	$2.50, breakfast • $5.00, lunch • $8.00, dinner
Discounts:	none offered
Catering:	no
House favorites:	seafood buffet
Other:	take-out orders available

Though you might associate the phrase "double your pleasure" with a chewing gum, it is quite possible that citizens of McCormick use it to describe a local restaurant: Edmunds' and Callie's on Main, the successful union of two former dining establishments.

This story begins with Callie Patterson. Callie had run restaurants for a number of years when her husband, Kenneth, suggested they move to Callie's hometown of McCormick. It seemed only natural, upon returning home, that she open a restaurant of her own.

Callie found an available building on Main Street and

opened for business, calling her place Callie's on Main. The restaurant featured breakfast, short orders, and a southern-style lunch buffet. It soon began building a customer base.

Callie's primary competition was another popular restaurant located just down the street: Edmund's Seafood.

An interesting business move presented itself to Callie in March 1997. The owner of Edmunds' Seafood called her and asked if she'd be willing to buy him out. Kenneth, who helps his wife in the restaurant several evenings each week, felt it was a good opportunity. "We knew we'd take our customers with us," he said, "and figured to keep most of his."

One advantage to taking over the competition was that Edmund's building was bigger. It had been built in 1920 and used as a movie theater until the late 1960s. From silent movies, using a hand-turned projector, to modern motion pictures, the building known as the Hollywood Theater provided entertainment for several generations: movies—musicals, comedies, mysteries, and westerns—and live stage shows.

Though Callie would now be owner of the new facility, she didn't want to lose Edmunds' existing customers. So she decided to combine the names of the two restaurants into one and continue the previous owner's most popular feature: the seafood buffet on Thursday, Friday, and Saturday. "I kept everything he had been serving and added some of my own things," Callie explained.

Among the offered dishes on the dinner buffet are fried, grilled, and boiled shrimp; catfish; deviled crab; stuffed clams; fried clams; fried chicken; fried fish fillets; and broiled fish. There is also a selection of fresh vegetables as well as hushpuppies, French fries, baked potatoes, a salad bar, and homemade dessert. The cost for this smorgasbord is $11.99.

Weight watchers may choose just the salad bar ($4.50); although, with the choices so generous, the word "just" doesn't seem quite appropriate. Crab salad, potato salad, pasta salad, coleslaw, fruit, and lettuce with all the fixin's, like pepperoni and cheese, make the possibilities almost limitless.

Should you wish to order off the menu, the home-cooked meals include chicken ($5.99), pork chops ($6.99), ribeye steak ($10.99), flounder ($7.99), shrimp ($7.99), and catfish ($7.99).

For lunch, entrees include shrimp platter ($6.99), hamburger steak ($4.99), grilled boneless chicken breast ($4.99), and barbeque ($4.99). On Sundays there is a limited buffet, with four meats and a variety of fresh cooked vegetables ($6.99).

Breakfast offerings include omelettes ($1.95–$3.50), biscuits and sandwiches (59¢–$1.25), and buttermilk pancakes ($1.95).

With the union of the two restaurants, Callie has had a tough job: keep two sets of customers happy in one restaurant. So far, she's been a good matchmaker.

Fannie Kate's Restaurant

Owner or manager:	Lou and Barbara Roberts
Address:	127 S. Main Street, McCormick
Directions:	From US 378 / SC 28 intersection down-town, follow SC 28 (Main Street) SE one block. Restaurant is on left.
Phone number:	800-965-0061
Hours of operation:	Restaurant: MON–FRI 11:00AM–2:00PM, 5:30–9:00PM; SAT 5:30–9:00PM
	Pub: MON–SAT 5:30PM–CLOSING (11PM–12AM)
	Hotel desk: 24 HOURS
Payment method:	major credit cards
Reservations:	not necessary, but preferred
Dress:	dressy casual
Gratuity:	included for parties of 6 or more
Bar:	pub
Alcohol:	yes
Diet/light menu:	chef's salad, broiled seafood
Children's menu:	yes
Average price for meal:	$5.00, lunch • $10.00, dinner
Discounts:	none offered
Catering:	no
House favorites:	ribeye, prime rib
Other:	smoking in pub only
	free breakfast for hotel guests

McCormick was once a railroad town. Train tracks ran alongside Main Street, and travelers and drummers (traveling salesmen) arrived and departed daily. These people often remained in town overnight and needed a place to stay. In 1882, the McCormick Temperance Hotel opened beside the railroad tracks, atop the old tunnels of the Dorn Mine.

A quaint, brick building with porches stretching across the front of the top and bottom floors, the hotel for years enjoyed a flourishing business. As automobiles began to replace the railroad as a means of transportation, passenger train service slowed, eventually ending, and the old hotel closed. Over time the building became dilapidated. It was about to be torn down when Barbara and Lou Roberts decided to save it.

Lou and Barbara were both school teachers. When the couple retired, they moved to McCormick, Barbara's hometown. But Lou was soon bored and, "In 1994, we decided to buy the old hotel, fix it up, and sell it," he said. "My wife is originally from McCormick. She and her parents used to eat here years ago.

"Teachers always complain about how busy their jobs keep them," Lou continued, "but actually they have a certain amount of free time. With my free time, I started working with contractors on the side." The Roberts put $750,000 into renovations on the old hotel, which included putting in fifteen bathrooms and a pub on the lower (basement) level. "It turned out very nice," Lou said, "and we are continuing to decorate."

The place turned out so nice, in fact, the two decided to keep it and run it as an inn and restaurant. They called the place Fannie Kate's, after the woman who last ran the hotel. Seven-year-old Fannie Kate had moved into the hotel in 1905 when her mother bought the hotel as a business and a home for her and her children. When Fannie Kate grew up, she took over the business, and local folks began to call the hotel by her name.

Fannie Kate's is now a showcase for mementos including the original hotel sign, which was discovered in an interesting way. One day, while in the hotel's storage shed, Lou had occasion to reach underneath the large wooden shelf. Looking up (on the shelf's underside), he noticed lettering: "McCormick Hotel." He quickly recognized the wooden sign he'd seen in old photographs of the hotel. Today, that sign hangs in the entrance hall to Fannie Kate's, alongside pictures and framed write-ups of the building's history.

"The thing that doesn't make sense about all this is that we decided to run a business we knew nothing about. However, we were able to attract three excellent chefs, and our food is outstanding," Lou said.

About ninety percent of the restaurant's customers come from the nearby Savannah Lakes resort housing area. People also come from Augusta (GA), Greenwood, and other outlying areas. "And we have some very loyal supporters right here in McCormick," Lou added.

The dinner menu includes such items as grilled pork loin ($11.95), blackened chicken breast ($10.95), shrimp alfredo ($10.95), chicken and broccoli ($9.95), and shrimp scampi ($13.95). "Our leader is ribeye for $13.95. We do our own butchering and the ribeye is wonderful," the proud owner said.

Fannie Kate's offers nightly specials—the most popular, the Friday and Saturday special: prime rib ($12.95). Another often-requested dish is grilled tuna steak ($11.95). "It's huge," Lou said.

For lunch, there are soups and sandwiches, such as fish

sandwich ($5.25) and patty melt burger ($4.95, with coleslaw, French fries, and tea). "Also for lunch," Lou said, "we have specials, such as spaghetti, country fried steak, and stew. And we have a dessert of the day made in our own kitchen."

In the pub you can get sandwiches or anything from the dining room menu.

"We're very flexible. If you want something that's not on the menu, just tell us and we'll try to fix it for you," Lou said.

The pub held Oktoberfest festivities for the first time in 1998. "Everyone had a grand time. Also, we just started having a classical guitarist in the dining room every Thursday evening," Lou said. "Things are really going well and business is good."

♦ Billy Dorn struck gold in McCormick County in the early 1850s. Tunnels from the old Dorn Mine still run under the town of McCormick.

Pee Dee

CHESTERFIELD COUNTY
Diane's Restaurant (Chesterfield)
Shiloh Fish Camp (Shiloh Community)
DARLINGTON COUNTY
The Beacon Restaurant (Hartsville)
B. J.'s Restaurant (Darlington)
DILLON COUNTY
King's Famous Pizza (Dillon)
FLORENCE COUNTY
Redbone Alley (Florence)
Schoolhouse Restaurant (Scranton)
LANCASTER COUNTY
Leigh Anne's Restaurant (Lancaster)
LEE COUNTY
Dixie Cafe (Bishopville)
MARION COUNTY
Little Pee Dee Lodge (Nichols)
Raspberries on Main (Marion)
MARLBORO COUNTY
The Whistle Stop Cafe (Clio)
SUMTER COUNTY
Big Jim's (Sumter)
Lilfred's (Rembert)

Diane's Restaurant

Owner or manager:	Diane Brewer and Kevin McCarthy
Address:	1225 W. Boulevard, Chesterfield
Directions:	Approaching town limits of Chesterfield on SC 9 from the E, take the bypass. Restaurant is at western end of bypass (about 2 miles) on left, across from Curtis Mini-Mart.
Phone number:	843-623-2577
Hours of operation:	MON–FRI 11:00AM–2:00PM
Payment method:	local checks
Reservations:	not needed
Dress:	casual
Gratuity:	not included
Bar:	no
Alcohol:	not served
Diet/light menu:	salads
Children's menu:	no
Average price for meal:	$5.00
Discounts:	none offered
Catering:	no
House favorites:	fried chicken, grilled chicken, desserts
Other:	dinner served one night per month

Experts are fond of saying that childhood experiences shape what we do as adults. In the case of Diane Brewer, I would have to agree. Some of her fondest childhood memories, she says, involve standing on a milk crate and flipping hamburgers at her uncle's drive-in restaurant.

With this upbringing, it is no surprise that Diane knew at an early age the career she wanted: to own a restaurant. Though she was only twenty-one and inexperienced—except for the childhood burger flipping—Diane was willing to take a chance when the opportunity presented itself.

"I had been looking around for a building in Chesterfield for some time but couldn't find anything suitable," she explained. "I was in Patrick [fifteen miles away] and drove by a building that was for sale. I thought it was perfect and ran home to my father screaming 'I've found a place! I've found a place!'"

In case you're confused about how finding a building in another town helped Diane, you need to know that the "building" was actually a trailer. While many people might wonder about turning a trailer into a dining establishment, Diane never had such doubts.

"A bank down there had used it and it was completely empty. I knew that we could build some walls, a kitchen, bathrooms—everything that I would need for a restaurant. After I found a vacant lot I was in business."

Her idea was evidently a good one. Diane's has been going strong since 1980. The trailer is much roomier inside than it appears from the outside. There is seating for nearly sixty. Diane now runs the place with her friend Kevin McCarthy, a native of New York. Kevin's background as a cook is a nice compliment to Diane's.

"Everything we cook in here is from scratch," she said. "I do things such as fried chicken, cornbread, and slaw. Kevin came in and started doing a number of pasta dishes and lasagna. The people who come in here have really begun to enjoy those items."

Diane's Restaurant is open for lunch Monday through Friday, 11:00 AM to 2:00 PM. She offers a daily special of one meat and several vegetables ($5.00). If you're still hungry after the first serving, just tell your waitress to bring you more. Diane also serves a number of sandwiches, such as Philly cheese and French dip, as well as a number of homemade desserts.

Though many people enjoy traditional hearty dishes, Diane herself is quite concerned about healthy cooking. She tries to prepare food in a fat-free manner if at all possible, and is quite proud of the grilled chicken salad she offers.

"I don't use fatback to cook with anymore. It's not healthy," she says. "I didn't really think I could do without using it, but I've found the food tastes just as good."

As an interesting bonus for her loyal clientele, Diane opens the restaurant one night a month when she prepares her famous prime rib. But don't look for any ads in the local paper about it. "When I decide to do it, I let my good customers and friends know about it," she said. "I have one seating for about fifty people and it fills up pretty quick. If you happen to wander in on that night, I'll take you as long as I have room."

If you think that all the good places to eat are in large fancy buildings and big cities, think again. Though you may be surprised to find a restaurant in a mobile home, you'll be even more surprised with the quality of the food.

♦ Jazz great Dizzy Gillespie hails from Chesterfield County.

Shiloh
Fish Camp

Owner or manager:	Mike and Johnnie McCright
Address:	SC 102, Shiloh community, near town of Chesterfield
Directions:	From Chesterfield, take SC 102 S for about 4 miles to Shiloh United Methodist Church. Restaurant is just past church on right.
Phone number:	843-623-7204
Hours of operation:	THU–SAT 5:00–10:00PM
Payment method:	major credit cards
Reservations:	not needed
Dress:	casual
Gratuity:	not included
Bar:	no
Alcohol:	not served
Diet/light menu:	no
Children's menu:	no
Average price for meal:	$7.00
Discounts:	none offered
Catering:	no
House favorites:	scallops

If one of the rules for being successful in business is to have a highly visible location, then one might say that Mike and Johnnie McCright weren't playing by the rules when locating their restaurant in the Shiloh community. The parking lot of their restaurant, Shiloh Fish Camp, is consistently full, however, despite its location.

The McCrights met at the University of South Carolina where Johnnie was a fine arts major and Mike was working on a degree in biology. Johnnie's father started the fish camp thirty-one years ago; in 1978, the couple decided to buy him out.

"My father-in-law, Ralph Wilson, started the business after he had been to North Carolina and had had to wait for over over an hour to eat at a fish camp," Mike explains. "There wasn't anything like that is this area, but he figured if they were that popular in North Carolina, they'd go over well here."

Even though the Shiloh Fish Camp is located in the middle of nowhere, this was not a deterent to Ralph. "The place that my father-in-law went to and had the long wait was also in the middle of nowhere," Mike said.

The McCrights' customers come from as far as 150 miles away. The fish camp has served families, truckers, blue-collar workers, and even a chief justice of the South Carolina Supreme Court (Chief Justice Woodrow Lewis was a fish camp regular for years).

Fish camps originally were located along rivers and were places where fishermen cooked and sold their catch. The term now sometimes applies to restaurants specializing in seafood.

The interior of Shiloh Fish Camp is rustic. The wooden tables seat 225 people, and on weekends may serve from 1200 to 1300 meals. Many of the items are fried. "We go through seventy-five to eighty gallons of peanut oil in a weekend," Mike said. But broiled and baked dishes are available.

Many of the meals are served in large and small portions. There's flounder (large, $6.50; small, $4.25), croaker (large, $6.75; small, $4.50), and shrimp (large, $7.95; small, $6.50), among other fish and seafood. If you want variety, try the seafood platter ($8.95), the flounder and shrimp dinner ($7.95), or a number of other combination dishes. The non-seafood menu includes chicken ($4.95), a sixteen-ounce T-bone steak ($8.95), and hamburger steak ($4.75).

The couple divides their duties at the restaurant into areas with which each is most comfortable. Johnnie looks after the kitchen (joined by their son who washes dishes), and Mike manages the dining room. Mike admits that their work is easier because of their dependable employees, many of whom have been with the place for over a decade.

The Beacon Restaurant

Owner or manager:	Madge Zemp
Address:	1731 N. Fifth Street, Hartsville
Directions:	US 15 runs through center of Hartsville. Follow US 15BUS N through town and across Prestwood Lake. After passing the lake, continue for about 1-3/4 miles. Restaurant is on right.
Phone number:	843-332-2022
Hours of operation:	MON–SAT 5:00–10:00PM
Payment method:	checks, major credit cards
Reservations:	recommended for large groups
Dress:	casual
Gratuity:	not included
Bar:	yes
Alcohol:	yes
Diet/light menu:	salads, grilled chicken
Children's menu:	yes
Average price for meal:	$15.00
Discounts:	none offered
Catering:	yes
House favorites:	filet mignon
Other:	private dining rooms available

Many children follow in the footsteps of their parents when deciding a career path. While Madge Zemp hasn't done that exactly, she has come pretty close.

Madge literally grew up in the restaurant business. Her parents started The Beacon in 1946. It has been prospering since that time, an amazingly long time in an industry where establishments come and go like the wind. It's certainly an indication that The Beacon must be doing something right.

As with many family-run businesses, Madge began working there when she was fourteen. She took over the operation of the facility in the early 1980s. Of course, with her background, she didn't need any training to run the place. "I had on-the-job training," she says.

While for her parents the restaurant was a full-time enterprise, Madge considers it only a hobby. Her primary job is that of high school teacher (ninth and eleventh grades). After teaching during the day, she oversees the restaurant in the evening. "It's a full-time hobby," she says. "My husband luckily supports it."

Fortunately for Madge, she has an excellent staff that allows her to leave the restaurant and feel confident that everything is progressing without her. Some of her absences are to accompany her husband. His job takes him around the world and, when school is out, she occasionally travels with him.

"My people carry on whether I'm there or not because we have very, very little turnover," she says with pride. Her cook has been at The Beacon for thirty-four years. Madge's husband also helps out in the kitchen. "Sid is a gourmet cook, so every weekend, in addition to our regular menu, we have 'Sid's Specials,'" she said.

The building is very rustic and from the outside looks like it dates back to pioneer days. But it was built right where it is as a restaurant. The inside is also rustic but not extremely so. "We have a lot of wood and wallpaper in nice, rich colors. It's sort of hard to describe the decor. You have to see it," Madge says.

In addition to the main dining room, there are several private dining areas that seat from four to one hundred people. There's also a bar you can enter from the back of the building. It's called Baron's Outback (You'll see the sign if you're trying to find it).

Steak is a favorite with customers of The Beacon. Prime rib and filet mignon are the biggest sellers. Other menu items include a seafood platter ($13.95), grilled chicken breast ($8.85), shrimp fettucine ($10.50), and pork chops ($10.95).

The dessert cart is a big treat, with the assortment changing daily. The only problem is deciding what to choose.

In business now for over half century, The Beacon is a favorite with residents of Hartsville and still going strong.

B. J.'s Restaurant

Owner or manager:	Belinda Bonnoitt, Judy Moore, and Lisa Ralley
Address:	1022 Pearl Street, Darlington
Directions:	From I-95, take US 52 (exit 164) NW about 5 miles to US 52 BYPASS. Follow BYPASS through 2 traffic lights; take next exit (at bridge) to right, Pearl Street. Restaurant is 1/10 mile on left, in Winn Dixie shopping plaza.
Phone number:	843-393-4957
Hours of operation:	MON–SAT 5:00AM–9:30PM
	SUN 6:00AM–9:00PM
Payment method:	major credit cards
Reservations:	not needed
Dress:	casual
Gratuity:	not included
Bar:	no
Alcohol:	not served
Diet/light menu:	salad bar
Children's menu:	yes
Average price for meal:	$4.00, breakfast • $7.00, lunch/dinner
Discounts:	none offered
Catering:	yes
House favorites:	fried chicken (lunch), prime rib (dinner)

As most South Carolinians know, Darlington is a mecca for stock car racing fans throughout the Southeast. With such great interest in the sport in this area, it is no wonder that one of the most popular restaurants in town has a racing theme.

That place is B. J.'s Restaurant, located on the road leading to its famous racetrack. Stock car enthusiasts are drawn there because of the racing theme. Pictures of famous drivers and models of stock cars decorate the place. The wallpaper border is from NASCAR and there are black-and-white checkered tablecloths.

If you are in Darlington during a race weekend, you might want to avoid B. J.'s. It becomes a virtual madhouse. But if you are in the area at other times, don't miss the place. It's open for breakfast, lunch, and dinner, seven days a week.

Three sisters own the restaurant: Belinda Bonnoitt, Judy Moore, and Lisa Ralley. No matter when you visit, they are there. When asked where the name of their business came from, Belinda explained, "The 'B' is for me and the 'J' is for Judy. Lisa's real name is Sherry Alicia; we tell her she's the little 's.'"

Belinda's statement is actually a family joke. The restaurant was started by the sisters' cousin, Bobby June—hence, the name B. J.'s. The sisters' father purchased the business from their relative.

"After Dad decided to retire, we bought it from him," Belinda said. "As it turns out, he got bored with retirement and has opened a restaurant in Summerton."

One of B. J.'s main features is its enormous soup and salad bar ($4.00) where you can get unlimited refills. Popular items from the menu include grilled chicken breast ($4.50), pork chops ($5.50), spaghetti ($4.50), a twelve-ounce New York strip ($7.95), and fried or sauteed shrimp ($5.95). There is also an assortment of daily specials.

Mornings, you can enjoy a real, down-home breakfast: hot cakes and waffles ($2.00–$3.75), omelets ($2.75–$3.75), or a biscuit with sausage gravy ($1.75). Eggs, bacon, and grits are also available.

On the front of B. J.'s menu is printed, "in memory of Carlene." Carlene was a fourth sister who died in November 1996.

King's
Famous Pizza

Owner or manager:	Nazmy Khalil
Address:	100 South Second Avenue, Dillon
Directions:	From I-95, take SC 34 (exit 190) W to downtown Dillon (about 2 miles), where it becomes Main Street. Follow SC 34 across RR tracks to US 301/501 (Second Avenue); restaurant at this intersection on right.
Phone number:	843-774-3811
Hours of operation:	MON–SAT 10:30AM–9:30PM
Payment method:	major credit cards
Reservations:	not needed
Dress:	casual
Gratuity:	not included
Bar:	yes
Alcohol:	yes
Diet/light menu:	grilled chicken salad
Children's menu:	no
Average price for meal:	$5.00, lunch • $8.00, dinner
Discounts:	none offered
Catering:	no
House favorites:	pizza, Greek salad
Other:	take-out available

At the corner of US Hwy. 52 and US Hwy. 301 stands a restaurant that looks very ordinary from the outside. If you ask residents of Dillon, however, you will discover this unassuming exterior masks one of the favorite spots for locals, popular for almost two decades.

The name of this place is King's Famous Pizza. Besides the name (anything with the word "famous" catches your attention), there isn't much that would attract you to this bistro in the heart of downtown—not from the outside anyway. It's located in front of a small shopping center, where two busy streets converge.

The restaurant is owned and run by Nazmy Khalil and his family. As you would suspect from his name, Nazmy is foreign—but he is not Italian (as the word "pizza" might suggest); he is Egyptian. In 1981, when he first opened King's, Nazmy knew that Dillon was much too small to support a place that specialized in Egyptian cuisine. But he knew most people enjoyed pasta and pizza.

Nazmy is almost always at his restaurant making sure everything runs smoothly. His family is a tight-knit unit and it isn't unusual to see one or more of his family members assisting him in whatever is needed.

One of the reasons King's is so successful is the very low turnover in their staff. While most restaurants do well to keep the same personnel in place for three months, many of King's workers have been employed for five to ten years. It is this continuity that allows the restaurant to maintain its level of excellence.

The interior of King's Famous Pizza isn't flashy, but comfortable. With its dim lighting and small, intimate booths, it has the feel of an old Italian restaurant. The reason for King's popularity isn't the decor, however; it's the food.

As you would have guessed, pizza is one of the top sellers on the menu. The crust is tossed fresh in the kitchen and customers are offered a variety of toppings. A large special (cheese, hamburger, pepperoni, Italian sausage, bell pepper, onion, and mushroom) sells for $13.99 and is usually enough to feed three to four people. If you and your lunch partner can't agree on toppings, you can each order a mini pizza ($2.49). For $3.99 you can get the mini pizza with a salad or appetizer and iced tea.

Nazmy offers a number of traditional Italian dishes in addition to pizza. The lasagna probably sells best, but there is also manicotti, ravioli, spaghetti, and chicken parmesan (lunch, $4.95; dinner, $7.95—includes a trip to the salad bar). If you like subs, the Super Sub would be a terrific choice. Filled with ham, turkey, roast beef, bacon, lettuce, and cheese, it is a meal

in itself for less than five dollars.

One of the most popular items at King's is not Italian at all. It's the Greek salad (lunch, $3.49; dinner, $4.50). The chicken salad (lunch, $3.49; dinner, $4.50) is a healthy choice and high in demand.

While Dillon County may be best known as the home of South of the Border, King's Famous Pizza is working to make the county well-known for something else as well: good Italian food at reasonable prices.

Redbone Alley

Owner or manager:	Dale Barth
Address:	1903 W. Palmetto Street, Florence
Directions:	I-20 E ends in Florence. From I-20/I-95 interchange, follow I-20 E about 2 mi.les to Evans Street (4th stop light). Just past 4th light, turn left into Florence Mall. Restaurant is behind Piggly Wiggly, on Palmetto Street side of mall.
Phone number:	843-673-0035
Hours of operation:	MON–SAT 11:30AM–12:00M SUN 11:30AM–9:00PM
Payment method:	major credit cards
Reservations:	recommended for large groups
Dress:	nice casual
Gratuity:	not included
Bar:	yes
Alcohol:	yes
Diet/light menu:	several items*
Children's menu:	yes
Average price for meal:	$10.00
Discounts:	none offered
Catering:	no
House favorites:	Low Country shrimp and grits, "dem bones" chicken
Other:	*menu evaluated by hospital; healthy choices marked

When most people want to open a restaurant, they get a building, install a kitchen, and put out some tables and chairs. Not Dale Barth. When he established Redbone Alley in Florence, he created an enclosed, miniature city.

"I've always loved eating at the little sidewalk cafes in Charleston," he said. "But, I didn't think that would work in Florence. It would be either too hot or cold, or there'd be flies." He came up with a plan to have a sidewalk cafe *inside*.

First, Dale selected a building. He bought the old JC

Penney store that was sitting empty. He knocked out a portion of the first-floor ceiling to open up the second story, creating a thirty-foot-high space. Next, he and his wife visited Charleston, Savannah, and New Orleans and took lots of pictures. They presented them to the architect, making only one request: "We want it to look like this."

The resulting design could not have been more perfect. The walls are painted with images of houses and shops, where pigeons perch on window sills. Attached to some houses are porches and balconies. An *alley* winds through the mock city and trees are situated throughout. The dining tables are placed along the twists and turns of the alley and on the porches and balconies. For kids, an ice cream truck filled with toys offers a play area and a cooler with ice cream bars for dessert. Customers can best appreciate the miniature city from the balconies.

In a room that connects to the restaurant, Dale added a bar for adults who just want a drink or to watch television while dining.

Upstairs, on the open second level, is a gameroom with video games and pool tables.

The entire place covers a whopping 20,000 square feet. Despite its size, there is a surprising sense of intimacy.

Dale had previous experience in the restaurant business,

having run Florence's most upscale eatery. "But my wife and I had started a family," he said, "and we realized how important it was to have a restaurant geared toward children. The other place was too expensive for families, and getting a babysitter made it a pricey evening for parents."

Dale's six-year-old daughter is credited with the name of the restaurant. "One day," he explained, "she came home with a redbone coon hound. She said, 'This dog's mine and his name is Clementine.' How can you say no to that?"

While the daughter wanted the restaurant to be called Clementine, they compromised and chose Redbone.

An image of the dog is the restaurant's logo. In the gift shop, you can buy shirts, hats, and other souvenirs with the red dog logo. The hound appears on the sign outside and on the menus. Also, a six-foot-tall redbone and a doggy friend are seated at a table on the highest balcony, keeping a watchful eye over the activities below.

There is even a letter from the dog to customers printed on the menus. He writes, "What's the secret to Redbone Alley? It's simple: good, fresh, innovative food; attentive and friendly service; and just plain fun. You don't have to be born with a silver bone in your mouth to figure it out."

The old dog is right! The restaurant is fun and the service is above the ordinary. Best of all, the food is top quality. You can get a three-way shrimp platter (six blackened, six grilled, and six fried) for $12.99; a mixed grill (beef, shrimp, and chicken) for $14.99; Jambalaya pasta for $10.99; and marinated ribeye for $14.99. Salads include grilled chicken with greens ($7.99), pecan salad ($7.99), and grilled shrimp and pasta ($9.59). There are a lot more meals and salads as well as a great selection of sandwiches and appetizers.

Because of the good food and entertaining atmosphere, Dale calls his business an "eatertainment." You won't find this word in Webster's Dictionary, but it is only because Webster never ate at Redbone Alley.

Schoolhouse Restaurant

Owner or manager:	Howell Myers
Address:	US Hwy. 52, Scranton
Directions:	US 52 runs through the tiny town of Scranton (about 3 miles N of Lake City; 16 miles E of I-95). Headed S on US 52, restaurant is on left, in center of town.
Phone number:	843-389-2020
Hours of operation:	THU–SAT 11:00AM–9:00PM SUN 11:00AM–2:00PM
Payment method:	checks
Reservations:	not accepted
Dress:	casual
Gratuity:	not included
Bar:	no
Alcohol:	not served
Diet/light menu:	salads
Children's menu:	reduced price for buffet ($4.00)
Average price for meal:	buffet, $6.00
Discounts:	none offered
Catering:	yes
House favorites:	barbecue, homemade biscuits

For years the solitary schoolhouse in the Florence County town of Scranton was filled with the noise and laughter of children. The students are no longer there, but the building is again filled with happy sounds, thanks to Howell Myers.

The building was constructed in the 1930s as a WPA project and served for thirty years as a school for black students. After it closed, the building sat empty, its only use that of storage for overflow items and junk from the furniture store of Howell's father.

Howell had worked for the railroad for twenty-five years when he was offered early retirement, with pension paid in a lump sum. The deal sounded good to Howell, who decided to use the money to renovate the old schoolhouse across the road from where his father's store had been and open up a restaurant.

"The first thing I had to do was restore the place," he said. "It was a mess. My brother said I'd never get it into good enough shape to use it for anything."

Despite the inherent difficulties of restoring a building of that age, Howell's faith was not shaken. He began work on the place by replacing windows and refinishing floors. Then, he added a large room on the back.

"I replaced 500 window panes. I sanded down all the frames, soaking them in lemon oil. I used gallons and gallons of the cleaner Purple Power, scrubbing everything," Howell reported, adding that he wouldn't do it again for anything.

He was lucky to have the help of his friend, Lee, who assisted as electrician and plumber. But Howell was anxious to open his restaurant. "Eventually," he said, "we decided we had to quit fussing around with the renovations. So we arbitrarily picked a day to open."

That day was May 26, 1994. As this was his first venture into the restaurant business, Howell admitted he didn't know what to expect. He hoped it would be slow at first until he learned the tricks of the trade. However, that isn't what happened.

"Right away," he said, "the place was busting at the seams. And it got even busier as the word spread. People are now coming from Myrtle Beach, Florence, Sumter, and even North Carolina."

While there is some interest in the building, the main attraction is the food. It's good, and there's plenty of it. There are two long buffet tables filled with barbecue, chicken, roast beef, collards, rice, peas, sweet potatoes, coleslaw, corn, homemade biscuits, and all the other dishes you'd expect to find on a southern dining table. The third counter displays a selection of desserts, such as pudding, cake, and ice cream. The best part may be the price. This unlimited extravaganza is just $6.00.

Besides the food, people enjoy the decor. There's a mural on one wall depicting Myers's Furniture Store (the former family business) and a train on the other. There is also a display case exhibiting all kinds of model trains.

A second room boasts a collection of toy trucks and cars. There are also shelves filled with tobacco tins and old blue medicine bottles. Framed advertisements from long-ago adorn the walls. "I'm a collector," Howell said. "I had a lot of this stuff before I had the restaurant."

The Schoolhouse is open Thursday through Sunday year-round, closed only when Christmas falls on one of those days. "My employees grumble a bit about working on Thanksgiving and other holidays, but they must not mind too much because most of the people I hired when I opened are still with me. Actually, I let the employees run all over me."

When asked to sum up his experience as a restaurateur, Howell said lightly, "It's been a trip!"

Leigh Anne's Restaurant

Owner or manager:	Marc Culler
Address:	200 N. Catawba Street, Lancaster
Directions:	Headed E on SC 9 from the Catawba River (Chester County line), go about 5 miles to town of Lancaster, where SC 9 becomes Catawba Street. Follow Catawba for 5 blocks to Meeting Street; restaurant on left at this corner.
Phone number:	803-285-6606
Hours of operation:	MON–THU 6:00AM–8:00PM FRI–SUN 6:00AM–3:00PM
Payment method:	checks
Reservations:	not accepted
Dress:	casual
Gratuity:	not included
Bar:	no
Alcohol:	not served
Diet/light menu:	chef's salad, cold plate
Children's menu:	child's plate available
Average price for meal:	$6.00
Discounts:	none offered
Catering:	yes
House favorites:	fried chicken, stuffing
Other:	popular Sunday lunch buffet

Twenty years ago, Margie Points was practically working herself to death as manager of a convenience store. One evening in 1980, after another long day at work, Margie made a decision: if she was going to work this hard, she might as well be doing it for herself. That's how Leigh Anne's Restaurant in Lancaster came into being.

Marc Culler, Margie's son, now runs the business but accredits its success to his mother. "Leigh Anne's was her brainchild. She's the one that should get all the credit for putting everything together. She was born in Lancaster but had moved away for about twenty years before returning. She didn't have any prior restaurant experience, but was motivated and driven to have a good restaurant."

One of the first things Margie had to do was choose a name for her new place. She picked something close to her heart. "Leigh Anne's is named for my sister, who was just a child at the time," Marc said. "Her portrait still hangs in the restaurant. Leigh Anne is now grown up, but she sometimes comes in."

Marc himself was an engineer for Duke Power for a number of years. Duke was trying to streamline their operations and offered a separation package to some employees if they would leave the company voluntarily. At around the same time Margie was looking for someone to take over the management of Leigh Anne's. Marc had always promised he would take care of it. He left his job as an engineer and "bought into the headaches" of the restaurant.

Though she turned over control to her son, Margie is still involved in the business. Marc says they work hard to stay consistently good. "Our crowd is a blue collar crowd. We don't

advertise; we rely on word of mouth. We know that if we don't do a good job everyday, people will go eat elsewhere."

Leigh Anne's big draw is the daily lunch special. For $4.50 you get one meat, three vegetables, cornbread, and tea. Of all the items offered, the fried chicken, dressing, macaroni and cheese, and potato salad are the big favorites. There are also a number of sandwiches, such as fish ($2.25), chicken filet ($2.25), and ham and cheese ($2.30). If you want something on the lighter side, there is a chicken salad cold plate ($3.75) and a veggie cold plate ($3.50). At breakfast there is traditional fare, such as pancakes, omelets, and biscuits.

Sunday is their busiest day. The Sunday lunch buffet offers four meats and fourteen vegetables from which to select, as well as dessert. Turkey, ham, and roast beef are often entrees at this meal.

Leigh Anne's had operated successfully for almost two decades when Marc stepped in, so he wasn't about to start making changes. "Some of the staff has been here for over ten years, and they know more about how things work than I do," he said. "I've learned a lot about the business since coming in. A restaurant is like a newborn baby: you want to show it off to everyone."

As locals of Lancaster can tell you, their expectations are met when they visit Leigh Anne's.

Dixie Cafe

Owner or manager:	Sam and Shirley Copeland
Address:	205 N. Main Street, Bishopville
Directions:	From I-20, take US 15 (exit 116) NE about 2 miles to downtown Bishopville, where US 15 becomes Main Street. Restaurant is on left, corner of Main and Council
Phone number:	803-484 -9148
Hours of operation:	MON–THU 6:00AM–2:30PM
Payment method:	local checks
Reservations:	not needed
Dress:	casual
Gratuity:	not included
Bar:	no
Alcohol:	not served
Diet/light menu:	salads, soups
Children's menu:	no
Average price for meal:	$3.00, breakfast • $5.00, lunch
Discounts:	none offered
Catering:	yes
House favorites:	vegetables

Sam and Shirley Copeland's dreams were like those of many looking for a new opportunity: move to a new place and start a business from scratch. They seemed to be following their blueprint when they found an old house in Bishopville, purchased it, and began restoring it with the intent of opening a restaurant. Luckily for them and the local community, things didn't work out exactly as planned.

"We were in the process of converting the downstairs of the house into the dining room," Sam said. "One day the cook from the Dixie Cafe came to see if we needed any help. He told us that the owners of the Dixie had decided to close down. The next thing I knew, Shirley was calling the realtor who was handling the property."

Though they were new to the area, the Copelands were familiar with the downtown restaurant. Located on Main Street in the heart of Bishopville, the Dixie Cafe had been a mainstay since brothers Nick and Johnny Johnson opened it in the 1930s. The old-fashioned neon sign hanging from the brick facade out front gave the place a nostalgic feel.

Sam went to check out the establishment and discovered a deal too good to pass up. "The people who owned the building really wanted to get someone in there," he said. "I asked about the price and they said the lease would be $450 a month including the kitchen equipment, tables, and chairs. It didn't take me long to realize that we might better change our plans."

The Copelands signed a lease and made plans to reopen the Dixie. Not being locals, they figured they had to try extra hard to impress the natives. They had no idea how well they would be accepted.

"The town was as excited about the Dixie Cafe reopening as we were," Shirley said. "Everyone has given us support and

really talked it up. From the first day the place was packed. We have one table in front that we call the 'town council' because all the local officials and businessmen of the town sit there. They probably conduct more business there than they do at their offices."

The busiest time is lunch, with the buffet ($4.95) being the main attraction. Served cafeteria style, it offers a selection of three meats and five vegetables. Unlike many places that have the same items day after day, Sam rarely cooks the same thing twice. "I like to keep them off-guard," he says. Patrons can also choose from a variety of sandwiches ($2.25–$3.25), homemade vegetable soup ($1.50), and homemade chili ($1.95). The owners are especially proud of their homemade desserts.

Breakfast is also affordable. You can fill up for less than four dollars.

Most customers tell the Copelands it doesn't matter what they serve because it is all good. Shirley carefully describes the cuisine at the Dixie Cafe as "homestyle cooking with a chef's flair."

♦ Bishopville is home to the South Carolina Cotton Museum.

Little Pee Dee Lodge

Owner or manager:	Durant Martin, Jimmy Devers, and Ell Devers
Address:	US 76, Nichols
Directions:	US 76 runs through the small town of Nichols (about 7 miles E of Mullins; less than a mile W of the Horry County line; and less than 10 miles SW of the NC border). Restaurant is on right, just W of town.
Phone number:	843-526-2101
Hours of operation:	MON–SAT 5:00–10:00PM
Payment method:	checks, major credit cards
Reservations:	recommended on weekends
Dress:	dressy casual
Gratuity:	not included
Bar:	yes
Alcohol:	yes
Diet/light menu:	grilled chicken, broiled seafood
Children's menu:	yes
Average price for meal:	$12.00
Discounts:	none offered
Catering:	yes
House favorites:	seafood
Other:	on-site motel

National statistics show that seven out of every ten small businesses fail. Defying the odds, the Little Pee Dee Lodge has been going strong now for over seventy-five years, and the future looks as rosy as the past.

Nestled alongside the Little Pee Dee River, the Lodge opened its doors as a roadside tavern and inn in 1920. A fire in 1928 forced the owners to rebuild. A second room, The Palmetto Room, was added in the 1940s when Thomas ("Mr. Tom") Snowden acquired the business. Many dances, receptions, marriage proposals, weddings, and other special events have taken place in the riverside restaurant over the years.

Durant Martin, Jimmy Devers, and Ell Devers purchased the Lodge in 1994. Although they wanted to update the place a bit, they knew they didn't dare make too many changes to the building that housed the oldest restaurant in continuous operation in the state. All changes made were in keeping with the history of the place, and special effort was made to keep the original layout.

"We updated the kitchen facilities and added a bar, but on the whole we kept things the way they had been. We didn't want to change much and have it lose its atmosphere," explained managing partner Durant, who had previously managed nightclubs in Myrtle Beach and Columbia before moving back to the area of his birth. "It took us a year to do everything like we wanted, and there are still a few other things we need to handle."

It doesn't take long after you walk through the front door to understand why some customers routinely come from as far away as seventy-five miles to dine at the Little River Pee Dee Lodge. There are two main dining areas downstairs and one upstairs, each with its own rustic charm. Many of the booths are in their original state (except for a few coats of paint). If you can get a table upstairs by the window, you should do so. This affords a nice panoramic view of the area. There is also outside dining on the porch, popular when the weather is good.

Seafood is the specialty of the house, but there is a fine selection of steaks, chicken, and sandwiches. Durant said they like to do a number of specialty items, such as crawfish and frog legs. The gator bites ($6.25), which is the tail of an alligator cut into small nuggets and fried or grilled, is one of the top appetizers. Little Pee Dee Lodge is one of the few places that provides personal tableside oyster shucking ($26.95). There is also a wide range of more traditional seafood entrees, such as shrimp ($11.95), red snapper ($12.95), stuffed flounder ($14.25), and scallops.

If you eat so much you feel you can't drive home, there's no need to worry. The new owners also remodeled the motel rooms located next to the restaurant. These eleven rooms are often in use, as the restaurant is used for banquets and receptions.

Though the restaurant seats 210 people, you will probably have a wait on weekends if you arrive without a reservation. If its popularity continues, there is no doubt Little Pee Dee Lodge, which bills itself as "America's Finest Riverside Restaurant," will one day celebrate its centennial.

♦ Marion County is named for Gen. Francis Marion, better known as the Swamp Fox, who so stealthily alluded the British during the Revolutionary War.

♦ South Carolina's total area covers about 31,000 square miles.

Raspberries on Main

Owner or manager:	Mark and Jeannie Guice, and Richie Richardson
Address:	229 N. Main Street, Marion
Directions:	Follow US 76 downtown to Main Street. Turn N onto Main; go about 8 blocks. Restaurant is on left, diagonally across from First Citizens Bank.
Phone number:	843-423-9229
Hours of operation:	MON 11:00AM–2:30PM; TUE–FRI 11:00AM–2:30PM, 5:00–9:30PM; SAT 5:00–9:30PM
Payment method:	major credit cards
Reservations:	recommended on weekends
Dress:	casual to dressy
Gratuity:	15% on groups of 7 or more
Bar:	yes
Alcohol:	yes
Diet/light menu:	several choices available
Children's menu:	no
Average price for meal:	$6.00, lunch • $12.00, dinner
Discounts:	none offered
Catering:	yes
House favorites:	pork loin, crab cakes, mashed potatoes

When Mark and Jeannie Guice were deciding on a name for their new restaurant, Mark offered an unusual suggestion: Framboise.

Mark described her reaction: "She asked me what it meant and I said it was the French word for raspberries. She said she didn't know how the locals of Marion would take to the name but she did like its English translation. I hadn't considered calling it 'Raspberries' but it sounded good. We decided to add the 'on Main' part so that people could easily find us."

With the opening of the Guices' restaurant, locals of Marion had a place to go for what co-owner Richie Richardson calls "food with an old Charleston flair." Before Raspberries opened, most people had to go to nearby Florence for upscale dining. That is the reason the Guices made their way to Marion.

"I was working in Myrtle Beach at the time," Mark explained, "and came through Marion. It is a really pretty town but looked like it needed a nice place for dining. Even though we weren't from Marion, we thought we had a great opportunity just waiting for us."

Though this is their first restaurant, Mark has an impressive background. He attended cooking school in Asheville and interned at the Biltmore House. He then worked for a chef in Atlanta who was voted the number two top chef in the country.

Partner Richie doesn't have the formal training Mark has but at the time they joined forces he had over twenty years experience in the restaurant business. Richie happened upon Raspberries not through good luck but, strangely, bad luck.

"I was out of work and broke," declared Richie. "I needed some money to eat and decided to bring some crystal I had to an antique store downtown to see if I could sell it. After they said no, I was walking down the street and saw a 'help wanted' sign in the window of this new restaurant. I came in, met Mark, and had a job."

This was just the beginning of Richie's good fortune. He subsequently received an inheritance and Mark asked him if he was interested in becoming a partner in the restaurant.

"I'll put our food up against anyone around," Richie said. "The word is getting around about us. Now, instead of people in Marion going to eat in Florence, people in Florence are coming here."

That is not hard to believe considering their menu. The most popular dinner entree is grilled pork loin stuffed with shrimp and vegetables and topped with raspberry sauce ($11.99). Selections also include barbeque, chicken, and pasta. All entrees include a house salad, fresh baked bread, fresh vegetables, and a choice of mashed potatoes, rice, or baked potato.

There is also a selection of soups and salads.

Both Richie and Mark say you have to try the mashed potatoes. "These aren't any ordinary mashed potatoes," Mark said. "These are spiced with garlic and mint. When we first opened, everyone wanted to get baked potatoes and we had to say, 'No. You've got to try the mashed potatoes.' Now almost no one gets anything but the mashed potatoes."

Lunch specials include the Monte Cristo ($4.95), the shrimp salad pita ($5.25), and the pizza of the day (with basil on a boboli crust, $7.95). And Richie says the crab cakes are as good as he has ever had.

Appetizers include baked mushrooms stuffed with crab meat ($4.95) and seafood scampi ($8.95).

The town of Marion may not have been ready for a restaurant with the name Framboise, but it was certainly ready for a place with outstanding food and atmosphere. With Raspberries on Main, it has both.

♦ The sweetest attraction to the town of Marion just might be the Russell Stover candy outlet.

The Whistle Stop Cafe

Owner or manager:	Carolyn Gardner and Connie Perkins
Address:	SC 9, Clio
Directions:	From Bennettsville, follow SC 9 SE about 7 miles to Clio (6 miles S of NC border). SC 9 continues through town; restaurant is downtown on right. [From I-95, take SC 9 (exit 193) NW about 15 miles to Clio.]
Phone number:	843-586-7421
Hours of operation:	MON–FRI 6:00AM–1:30PM, SAT 7:00–10:30AM
Payment method:	local checks
Reservations:	not needed
Dress:	casual
Gratuity:	not included
Bar:	no
Alcohol:	not served
Diet/light menu:	salads, grilled chicken
Children's menu:	no
Average price for meal:	$4.00
Discounts:	none offered
Catering:	yes
House favorites:	grilled chicken salad, hamburger steak
Other:	extensive catering business

The movie *Fried Green Tomatoes* focuses on two women who decide to start a new career by opening a restaurant called The Whistle Stop Cafe in their small hometown. When you next visit Marlboro County and pass through the town of Clio, you'll think you have found a case of life imitating art.

In the heart of this town is a restaurant called The Whistle Stop Cafe. After finding out that the two owners are women who decided to try something new, you'll wonder if you have stumbled onto a Hollywood set. But Carolyn Gardner and Connie Perkins, the owners, are not former actresses, but nurses. The story behind their starting a restaurant together is certainly unique.

"We were working as nurses for a hospice and my son announced he was getting married," Connie explained. "So the two of us decided to cater it ourselves. We enjoyed doing that wedding and thought that it would be fun to open a catering business on the side. After some time it became obvious that we couldn't do this right just out of our home kitchens, we needed a building of our own. Then it just seemed natural that if we were going to have to pay for an additional building, we might as well use it as much as possible. That's how the restaurant came about."

Although both women had seen the movie, it was not the sole inspiration for choosing the name.

"The train tracks run right through the center of town. Years ago, Clio was one of the major places in the area that people went shopping. Each day the train would pull up in town and bring people to Clio. At the end of the day the train would return to pick up the shoppers. So we thought this was a good tribute to the town," Connie said.

The women decided they would offer good food at affordable prices. Open for both breakfast and lunch, the most expensive thing on the menu is the barbecue plate at just $4.00. The hamburgers and cheeseburgers, all made fresh, sell for less than $2.00 apiece. A number of salads (such as grilled chicken salad, $3.50), and soups ($2.50) are also offered. Breakfast fare is equally reasonable ($2.75), for one egg, bacon, grits, and biscuits. And how many places have coffee for thirty-five cents and tea for just fifty cents?

Because the restaurant opens only for breakfast and lunch on weekdays and breakfast on Saturday, Connie and Carolyn can use their facility to host catered affairs in the evenings and on weekends. That side of the business, which they call Carolina Caterers, has been growing steadily.

While Clio might be a small town, it was definitely in need of a restaurant for local citizens. If Connie and Carolyn keep on their current path, it won't be long before people in surrounding areas discover that The Whistle Stop doesn't have anything to do with trains but everything to do with good food.

♦ The Marlboro County town of Blenheim is home to South Carolina's very own, very spicy Blenheim Ginger Ale.

Big Jim's

Owner or manager:	Jim Karveles
Address:	451 Broad Street, Sumter
Directions:	US 378 becomes Broad Street in the town of Sumter. Entering town from the W, follow Broad past Jessamine Mall. At fourth traffic light, restaurant is on left.
Phone number:	803-773-3343
Hours of operation:	MON–SAT 7:00AM–10:00PM
Payment method:	major credit cards
Reservations:	recommended for main dining room
Dress:	nice casual
Gratuity:	not included
Bar:	yes
Alcohol:	yes
Diet/light menu:	salads, chicken dishes
Children's menu:	no
Average price for meal:	$5.00, lunch • $12.00, dinner
Discounts:	none offered
Catering:	in-house only—private dining rooms
House favorites:	steaks, seafood

Broad Street in Sumter is like many commercial thoroughfares common in today's expanding cities. As far as the eye can see, there are strip malls and neon signs. It was a pleasure to find, nestled in this strip of commercialism, a place that hasn't changed much in decades: Big Jim's.

Big Jim's has been going strong since 1955 and doesn't appear to be slowing up at all. While owner Jim Karveles can't point to just one reason for his success, he gives some credit to his heritage. "I'm Greek," he says. "Greeks know about good food."

It is interesting to note that Jim is just one of many Greeks who have been successful in America in the restaurant business. Besides knowing good food, Greek owners like Jim willingly sacrifice their free time for the sake of their business.

Jim's place is definitely a full-time enterprise. It is like three restaurants rolled into one. In the rear of the building is a coffee shop. The coffee shop, which has the feel of an old diner, serves primarily breakfast and lunch. The most popular time at the coffee shop is lunch, when a buffet ($5.95) attracts a mix of blue and white collar customers. There are also home-made hamburgers($4.00–$5.00), a chicken breast sandwich ($4.00), and a triple decker sandwich ($4.00) on the menu.

In front of the restaurant on the left side of the building is Big Jim's lounge. It has its own entrance, though you can get to it from inside the restaurant. The lounge has a darker, cozier feel, for those customers who want to stop by for happy hour or grab a quick drink before dinner.

The remainder of the building is Big Jim's main dining area. The restaurant's menu offers a broader range of selections than the other two sections. Fresh seafood and steaks (Jim does his own cuts) are favorites of customers. Seafood selections include the seafood platter ($14.95), scallops ($14.95), Maryland crabcakes ($10.95), and stuffed jumbo shrimp with pasta ($14.95). The steaks include Jim's famous ribeye (nine-ounce, $9.95; sixteen-ounce, $14.95) and the filet ($14.95) If you don't want beef or seafood, you could try the veal chops ($15.95) or the Greek chicken ($10.95). No matter what you get, save room for the South Carolina Mud Pie. This wonderful dessert is a coffee ice cream pie with chocolate graham cracker crust, topped with hot fudge and whipped cream ($3.50).

With over forty years of service, it is no wonder most Sumter residents are familiar with Big Jim's. The restaurant is now a popular stop for Canadian golfers who come to South Carolina in the winter to try our courses.

Whether you want a buffet lunch, a quick drink, or a fine dining experience, Big Jim's can satisfy all your desires.

Lilfred's

Owner or manager:	Mike Jones
Address:	US 521, Rembert
Directions:	The tiny town of Rembert is situated on US 521 about halfway between Camden and Sumter. The restaurant is one of the few buildings in town. You can't miss it.
Phone number:	803-432-7063
Hours of operation:	WED–SAT 5:00M–10:00PM
Payment method:	major credit cards
Reservations:	recommended on weekends
Dress:	casual to dressy
Gratuity:	not included
Bar:	yes
Alcohol:	yes
Diet/light menu:	ask waitress for light specials
Children's menu:	no
Average price for meal:	$15.00
Discounts:	none offered
Catering:	yes
House favorites:	Black Angus filet, quail, coleslaw, home-made croutons

The stretch of US Hwy. 521 between Sumter and Camden is the kind of highway you hope you don't break down on. There are very few houses and the landscape is made up of hay fields and woods. The only dot on the map is the tiny town of Rembert, a farming community that has been in decline over the last few decades.

Considering this, you will be surprised—no, amazed—to find that one of the two businesses in Rembert is an upscale restaurant whose owner studied cooking in France. While Lilfred's restaurant has been in operation since 1951, a first-time visitor is taken aback to find a place like this situated in relatively empty countryside. Not everyone thought owner Mike Jones was doing a smart thing when he bought the place nine years ago.

"There was a real split," he said. "Some of my friends thought I was crazy, while some said I had a great opportunity. I grew up in the area and was familiar with this place and thought I could bring it back to its glory."

Lilfred's had originally been opened by Lillian and Fred Kennemer and rose to popularity in the 1950s and '60s. It was billed as "South Carolina's Most Famous Little Restaurant" and was known for its frog legs, coleslaw, and homemade croutons. It happened to be for sale in the late '80s at the same time Mike was looking to open his own restaurant. His reasons for purchasing Lilfred's were simple: he didn't have much money and it was being sold cheap.

There aren't many restaurant proprietors in South Carolina who have the culinary background the friendly and outgoing owner of Lilfred's has. But it was actually a love of polo that initially got Mike into the business.

"I was playing polo one day and saw this guy pull up with a great horse trailer, beautiful horses, and a bunch of girls," Mike explained. "I wanted to find out what this guy's story was. I found out he was in the restaurant business in Charleston."

Mike met the fellow and was soon on his way to Charleston to work in one of the man's restaurants. Mike explained to his new boss that he wanted to start in the kitchen first so that he could learn the nuts and bolts of the business before moving to the floor. He quickly discovered a love for cooking and hasn't left the kitchen since.

The Charleston restaurant owner came to work one day with a problem. "One of his chefs at a restaurant he owned in Albertville, France, had left and they needed an immediate replacement," Mike explains. "He said I would be leaving in one week. I would be given free room and board and paid $15.00 a week. In return I would learn the art of cooking. I was there for nine months, and the experience was incredible."

After returning to the States he continued learning about

cooking and developed a keen knowledge of wine. From the first day of work, Mike knew he wanted to own his own place. When the chance to buy Lilfred's came up, he sprung at the opportunity. But he knew he couldn't make drastic changes to a place with such a long standing tradition.

"I knew there were some things I would have to keep— the coleslaw for one—because the customers were so used to it. About half of the current menu consists of items that I have added, about half are from the original menu from the '50s."

Since Mike took over the restaurant, it has been written up in a number of newspapers and magazines including *Gourmet* and *Charleston* Magazine. The Black Angus filet ($16.95), the sauteed quail with green peppercorn sauce ($15.95), and Lilfred's Ribeye ($16.95) are three of the most popular items. Any dish with sauce is highly recommended, as that is one of the hallmarks of Mike's French training.

Another surprising aspect of Lilfred's is the wine list. While most upscale places offer a dozen choices—which may or may not be in stock when you visit—Mike offers a virtual wine cellar, with 150 to 200 bottles in his wine closet at all times. And he believes in quality, not merely quantity. "We may not have the absolute largest selection of any restaurant in the state," he says, "but I've been told by many people that our collection is the best quality in South Carolina."

With Lilfred's in the area, perhaps breaking down on the lonely stretch of highway in the farming community of Rembert wouldn't be so bad after all.

Coastal

BEAUFORT COUNTY
    Reilley's (Hilton Head)
    Sgt. White's Diner (Beaufort)
    Shrimp Shack (St. Helena Island)
BERKELEY COUNTY
    Berkeley Restaurant (Moncks Corner)
CHARLESTON COUNTY
    Bowens Island Restaurant (Folly Beach)
    Hyman's Seafood Company (Charleston)
    The Old Post Office Restaurant (Edisto Island)
    Pinckney Cafe and Espresso (Charleston)
    SeeWee Restaurant (Awendaw)
COLLETON COUNTY
    Olde House Cafe (Walterboro)
DORCHESTER COUNTY
    Eva's Restaurant (Summerville)
GEORGETOWN COUNTY
    Flo's Place (Murrells Inlet)
    Rice Paddy (Georgetown)
    River Room (Georgetown)
HORRY COUNTY
    Alice's Café (Socastee)
    Boots' and John's Biscuit Shack (Cherry Grove)
    Grandma's Kitchen (Myrtle Beach)
    Mr. Fish (Myrtle Beach)
    Rivertown Bistro (Conway)
    Sea Captain's House (Myrtle Beach)
WILLIAMSBURG COUNTY
    T. Jarrett's Marker and Horn (Kingstree)

Reilley's

Owner or manager:	Tom Reilley
Address:	7D Hilton Head Plaza, Hilton Head Island
Directions:	Follow US 278 (only road onto the island) until it ends at Sea Pines traffic circle (10-1/2 mile drive from island bridge). Follow circle to Hilton Head Plaza on the left. Restaurant is in Plaza.
Phone number:	843-842-4414
Hours of operation:	7 DAYS A WEEK 11:30AM–2:00AM
Payment method:	major credit cards
Reservations:	not accepted
Dress:	casual to dressy
Gratuity:	included for large groups
Bar:	yes
Alcohol:	yes
Diet/light menu:	yes
Children's menu:	yes
Average price for meal:	$6.00, lunch • $9.00, dinner
Discounts:	seniors and PGA members
Catering:	no
House favorites:	cottage pie, corned beef and cabbage, fish and chips
Other:	big St. Patrick's Day celebration

What would you do if you were fired from your job, with four kids to support and a mortgage payment to make? When Tom Reilley was faced with this scenario, his decision seemed like a risky one: he opened his own restaurant.

Fifteen years later the wisdom in his move is obvious. Reilley's restaurant and pub on Hilton Head Island is firmly established with the local residents.

The decision, however, was not entirely Tom's. "I found the place and had the chance to get it for a great deal, but I really didn't want to do it. It was my wife who wanted us to buy it. She's the one who had the dream for the place, not me,"

Tom admits.

The restaurant can best be described as a cross between an Irish pub and a sports hall of fame. The interior is equally divided between a sit-down dining area on the right side and a large bar on the left. Tom, whose grandparents came from Ireland, points out that a native of that country would consider his establishment more in the style of an English pub than an Irish one.

One thing Reilley's has over an authentic Irish pub is good food. The most popular item is the cottage pie ($7.75). Tom says the recipe is an old family secret given to him by a relative from the old country. Corned beef and cabbage ($5.95), and fish and chips ($8.95) are also favorites among the locals who like the change from traditional American fare. Reilley's menu is fairly extensive. In addition to the Irish dishes, selections include seafood, hamburgers, chicken, and salads ($5.00–$8.00). Even the pickiest eaters will find something to their liking at Reilley's.

Sports junkies should visit this place just to see the large collection of sports memorabilia on display. Originally from Rhode Island, Tom has always been a big hockey fan. He shows his support by displaying autographed jerseys from Wayne Gretsky, Mark Messier, Mario Lemieux, and Bobby Orr. Larry Bird has visited the restaurant on different occasions and donated several items. You can also find autographs of Magic Johnson, Bob Cousey, and Rick Pitino. One of Tom's most prized pieces is a bat autographed by Willie Mays, which was actually given to his young son. While the son probably isn't happy about it, Tom thought it best to keep it in a display case at the restaurant instead of taking it to Little League practice.

Those who like to watch sports on television will also find Reilley's to their liking, as there are ten TV sets scattered throughout the bar area, broadcasting various sporting events. During football season groups often rent out the private room to watch their favorite teams in action. If you are ever on the island during St. Patrick's Day, be sure to stop in. Tom de-

scribes Reilley's special events this way: "It is a great week that day!"

On one occasion the restaurant donated lunch to Secret Service agents on the island with President Bill Clinton. The President sent a personal, handwritten note of thanks to Tom for his good will. This too is displayed near the bar.

Since opening his first location, Tom has since opened a second restaurant on the north end of the island. Just recently he was approached by a group that had visited his restaurant and liked it so much they asked if he would be interested in putting one on Maui. Tom made the deal and now has a good reason (not to mention a nice business deduction) to visit Hawaii.

While most restaurants on the island cater to the tourist crowd, this owner says the majority of his customers are locals. He sums up the reason for his success in one sentence: "Our view is that we are in the people business, not necessarily the restaurant business."

Sgt. White's Diner

Owner or manager:	Ron White
Address:	1908 Boundary Street, Beaufort
Directions:	Follow US 21 past Marine Corps Air Base. Continue 5 miles (past county government complex) to Piggly Wiggly (on the right). Restaurant is in front of Piggly Wiggly. (US 21 becomes Boundary Street in town.)
Phone number:	843-522-2029
Hours of operation:	MON–FRI 11:00AM–6:30PM
Payment method:	checks
Reservations:	not needed
Dress:	casual
Gratuity:	not included
Bar:	no
Alcohol:	not served
Diet/light menu:	no
Children's menu:	no
Average price for meal:	$5.50
Discounts:	none offered
Catering:	yes—weddings, barbecues
House favorites:	fried pork chops

Many restaurant owners worry about failure when opening up a new business. But after surviving a terrorist's bomb in his previous cooking job, Ron White had so such fears when he decided to open his place in Beaufort.

White, who is known as Sergeant White to everyone, knew from an early age he wanted to be in the food service industry. Upon graduating from school, he embarked on an unusual apprenticeship. He went down to his local Marine recruiting office and told them he would sign up for the service as long as they would teach him how to cook. While his fellow enlistees were sent for training in various areas of warfare, White was sent to cooking school, finishing first in his class.

He was soon preparing meals for up to five thousand Marines at a time.

While stationed at Parris Island, White fell in love with the Carolina Low Country. "I married a local girl and really liked the people I met," he said. "Though I knew I would be moved around with the military, I believed I would eventually come back to Beaufort."

After fourteen years in the Marine Corps, White decided he would finish out his twenty-year career in the service. He was sent to Beirut, Lebanon, to feed the U.S. troops stationed there. His plans changed when a terrorists' bomb hit the facility where he was working, killing many Americans. White, who was preparing a meal at the time of the attack, was seriously injured and forcibly discharged as a result.

The military's loss was the gain of hungry eaters in the Beaufort area. After taking additional cooking classes at Johnson & Wales in Charleston (to acquire some "finishing touches"), Ron decided to open his own place. He bought an old cinder block building, rebuilt the interior himself, and opened up Sgt. White's Diner. The food, which a *New York*

Times critic called a combination of "country cooking and soul food," draws people from all walks of life.

"Almost all my recipes come from my family in Tennessee. I don't serve anything that is canned or frozen. Everything comes from local farmers. I serve everyone from lawyers to policemen and construction workers," White states with pride.

Dinners that include one meat and two vegetables, cornbread, and drink sell for $5.50. While the menu changes based on the season, the following choices are usually available: smothered steak, pork chops, chicken, meatloaf, barbecue, fish, gumbo, mashed potatoes, yams, squash, local greens, and macaroni and cheese. Everyone, the owner claims, saves room for a slice of his sweet potato pie ($1.50).

While the local community has known about his place for years, it got an unexpected boost several years ago when a travel writer from the *New York Times* came in to eat lunch. She was so impressed with the place she wrote about it in a newspaper article. White says he is still amazed at the number of people from the North who came in afterwards and said they read about his place in that newspaper article.

Sgt. White's Diner is open Monday through Friday—with the lunch crowd on Fridays generally reaching over 200 people. White caters on weekends.

After all his years in the business, it is evident that Ron White isn't afraid of hard work. "A lot of people in this business want the easy way out," he says. "They serve everything out of cans and heat it up in the microwave. But I do everything from scratch. I don't mind sweating to make a living."

Shrimp Shack

Owner or manager:	Hilda Upton
Address:	1929 Sea Island Pkwy., St. Helena Island
Directions:	From bridge at Bay Street in Beaufort, follow US 21 15 miles. Shrimp Shack is on left, just before Harbor River bridge. (From Beaufort, you will cross 2 bridges. If you find yourself on Hunting Island, you've gone too far.)
Phone number:	843-838-2962
Hours of operation:	SPRING and SUMMER 11:00AM–8:00PM
Payment method:	cash only
Reservations:	not needed
Dress:	very casual
Gratuity:	not included
Bar:	no
Alcohol:	not served
Diet/light menu:	no
Children's menu:	child's plate available
Average price for meal:	sandwich, $3.00 • plate, $7.95
Discounts:	none offered
Catering:	no
House favorites:	shrimp burger, flounder sandwich, fried shrimp
Other:	non-seafood items available

Standing in front of Shrimp Shack on St. Helena Island, it's easy to imagine yourself in the setting of a Pat Conroy novel—herons walking through saltwater marshes, Spanish moss swaying from hundred-year-old oaks, the Carolina breeze cooling the summer heat. But Shrimp Shack is not a make believe place nor a prop in a Hollywood movie. It has been a favorite eatery among Low County residents for nineteen years.

Hilda Upton is part of a shrimping family. "My father was a shrimper," she says, "and my husband is a shrimper. Even though there were a good number of shrimpers back when we

started [1978], there was not a single restaurant in Beaufort that served locally caught shrimp. So we came up with the idea to open our own place that would serve shrimp caught right off our boats."

Thus, Shrimp Shack was born. Ms. Hilda thought it would be just a part-time enterprise during shrimping season, so they built only a small "shack" with a window where customers could place orders. Over the years the site has expanded from its humble beginnings. While you still place your order at the window, there is now a large screened porch, to accommodate customers who want to eat on the premises, as well as outside seating and a gazebo. The shack became so successful, it is now a year-round enterprise, though the hours are reduced during the winter.

The most popular item on the menu is the shrimp burger ($2.75). The flounder sandwich is another popular choice ($3.75). For those with larger appetites, there are a number of dinner choices: shrimp ($7.95), scallops ($8.10), deviled crab ($7.95), and clams ($6.10). Non-seafood items, such as hamburgers ($2.95) and chicken ($4.75) are available for landlubbers.

Besides being a source of family income, the restaurant

provided work for the Upton children as they were growing up. "The kids were always looking for summer jobs," Ms. Hilda says, "and since that time of year is our peak season, there was plenty of work for them. Now they are grown, but we still employ many local kids in the restaurant."

The restaurant has caught the attention of many people who have visited the area, and has been written up several times in the *Atlanta Journal-Constitution* and appeared in the premiere issue of *Coastal Living*, a new magazine from the editors of *Southern Living*. Shrimp Shack's popularity is shared equally between the area tourists and locals. A native of the island, having grown up across the road from the restaurant, Ms. Hilda regularly sees old school classmates and acquaintances. But she says the restaurant has given her the opportunity to make new friends with people who have recently moved into the area.

Shrimp Shack's popularity has not been lost on the many movie personalities who have come to the Low Country to make films, though Ms. Hilda refuses to name who exactly has eaten at her restaurant. "We know they like to be left alone, so no one bothers them when they come out here. Plus, we have a lot of people who are famous in their own right such as teachers and missionaries who we appreciate as much as any movie star."

Hollywood has made a number of movies depicting life in the Low Country of South Carolina. But if you want to experience the real thing, Shrimp Shack is a good place to start.

Berkeley Restaurant

Owner or manager:	W. J. and Rose Blackmon
Address:	399 US 52 N, Moncks Corner
Directions:	Restaurant stands at intersection of US 52 and US 17ALT.
Phone number:	843-761-8400
Hours of operation:	7 DAYS A WEEK 6:00AM–9:00PM
Payment method:	major credit cards
Reservations:	not needed
Dress:	casual
Gratuity:	not included
Bar:	no
Alcohol:	beer and wine
Diet/light menu:	seafood, chicken
Children's menu:	yes
Average price for meal:	buffet, $4.99 • menu meal, $12.00
Discounts:	10% to seniors
Catering:	yes
House favorites:	fried chicken, country ham with redeye gravy, pecan pie
Other:	private party rooms available

W. J. and Rose Blackmon have done a lot together over the past thirty years. Husband and wife have been best friends and business partners. Together, they manage the Berkeley Restaurant in Moncks Corner.

The Berkeley is much more than just a restaurant. "This place includes a seventy-two-room motel as well as a large restaurant," Rose explains. The Blackmons initially shared the chores in the restaurant, but W. J. has partially retired. "He still comes in and works but he calls himself the bus boy," Rose remarks.

The Berkeley Restaurant was opened in 1942, and the Blackmons purchased it from the original owners in 1972. Longevity seems to be a trend at the restaurant. Catherine Wren

has been employed there for thirty years and Katherine Blackmon (no relation to W. J. and Rose) is in her twenty-seventh year.

Even the customers seem to stay around a long time. Pervis Scott has been a regular for over twenty years. "I work for the phone company and I come by a lot for lunch. And I have breakfast with my daughter here on Sundays," he said, adding that he especially likes the Berkeley's chicken bog and brown rice. [Incidentally, this same Scott family was honored as South Carolina's Family of the Year a few years ago.]

Moncks Corner's close proximity to both Lake Moultrie and the Francis Marion National Forest means the area is a mecca for hunters and fishermen. Over time most of these gamesmen find their way to Berkeley Restaurant. Catherine Wren pointed out that some of the same deer hunters have been visiting the restaurant for over thirty years.

The motto of the place is simple: if you eat at the Berkeley often enough you'll see everyone in town. Rose says it is a spot where people come in to meet friends. "I know just about everyone in town from working at the restaurant,"

Catherine added.

The Berkeley does it all. The employees will even pack you a picnic lunch. They cater and offer three private dining rooms for receptions, business dinners, and private parties. And, of course, there is the restaurant itself and its variety of food.

Lunch is served buffet style ($5.95). There is an a la carte menu for breakfast and dinner. Menu items include a fourteen-ounce hunter's steak ($14.99), fried shrimp ($13.99), a seafood platter ($14.99), and a ten-ounce ribeye ($11.99).

Appetizers include shrimp cocktail, fried cheese sticks, hot wings, and chicken fingers (each $4.99). Sandwiches range from $2.50 to $5.00. There is also she crab soup ($3.50) and Lake Moultrie catfish stew ($2.99).

Through the years, the friendly atmosphere at the Berkeley has remained the same. Other things, however, have changed. Moncks Corner has grown from a handful of restaurants to the current thirty-one. Even with the increase, the locals still come to the Berkeley when they want to see friends and enjoy a good meal.

Bowens Island Restaurant

Owner or manager:	Robert Barber
Address:	1870 Bowens Island Road, James Island
Directions:	From intersection of SC 30 and SC 171 (Folly Road) on James Island, follow SC 171 S 5-1/2 mi. to Bowens Island Road. Turn right; road ends at restaurant.
Phone number:	843-795-2757
Hours of operation:	MON–THU 6:00–10:00PM
	FRI–SAT 5:00–10:00PM
Payment method:	major credit cards
Reservations:	not accepted
Dress:	casual
Gratuity:	not included
Bar:	no
Alcohol:	beer and wine
Diet/light menu:	no
Children's menu:	no
Average price for meal:	$10.00
Discounts:	none offered
Catering:	private parties in dock house
House favorites:	fried shrimp

When people think of the most unique restaurants in Charleston, they wouldn't imagine that one of them is located in a concrete block building at the end of a dirt road filled with ruts and potholes. But that is exactly the case with Bowens Island Restaurant.

Stately old oaks with hanging Spanish moss guide you along the dirt road. You will no doubt be mystified by your first look at the shabby building with odds and ends (junk) piled around it. It may take a bit of courage to get out of your car and enter the place. Yet for those with a fanciful turn of mind, it's a wonderful adventure.

Fifty years ago May Bowen saw a newspaper ad listing the thirteen-acre island for sale. She and her husband bought

it, displacing a herd of goats and several stills in the process. The couple built a road through the marsh and added a pier. Soon, fishermen began stopping by, asking if they had anything to drink; so the Bowens decided to stock a cooler with soft drinks to sell. Before long, fishermen began to ask May if she would consider preparing their daily catch; she agreed to cook for them. That proved to be such a success, the couple began to think about cooking full-time for the public. It wasn't long after, the Bowens had a restaurant on their hands.

Robert Barber, the Bowens' grandson, now owns the place. As a kid, he helped out, shucking oysters and peeling shrimp. When he grew up he became a minister in North Carolina and later a lawyer. He also served six years in the North Carolina legislature. Robert always assured his grandmother he would see to it the restaurant continued after she could no longer run it. He kept his word.

On the evening I visited the restaurant, Robert was on his way to a fancy party, running around in a tuxedo, an incongruous sight in a restaurant furnished with what looks like rejects from a Salvation Army thrift store.

"I told those people on the porch, 'I'll be your waiter tonight,'" Robert said, laughing at his own joke.

New customers are often surprised at what they find at Bowens. With its unusual decor—walls covered with graffiti, a 1948 jukebox, a beauty shop hair dryer, and an old grocery scale—it's hard to believe grown-ups decorated the place. After your eyes adjust, you find that it all actually adds to the restaurant's uniqueness.

The menu is what draws the crowds. Selections include roasted oysters (all you can eat, $14.50), fish and shrimp ($8.00), Big Ol' Seafood Platter ($14.50), Frogmore stew $9.00), shrimp and grits ($9.00), fish and grits ($8.00), and fried chicken ($5.95).

With its out-of-the-way location and rustic appearance, you might think there would be few customers. This, however, couldn't be farther from the truth. In fact, Bowens has been featured nationally in newspapers and magazines, and on television shows.

Robert told me a story about a restaurant reviewer who was known for her caustic pen. "She ordered some shrimp and grits and she ate every bit. I was going to take a picture of the plate but it got washed before I could get my camera. I figured that if she wrote a bad review, I'd produce the picture and say, 'You seemed to like the food well enough.'"

Hyman's Seafood Company

Owner or manager:	Eli Hyman
Address:	215 Meeting Street, Charleston
Directions:	Between Hayne and Pinckney Streets.
Phone number:	843-723-6000
Hours of operation:	MON–THU 8:00AM–11:00PM
	FRI–SUN 7:00AM–11:00PM
Payment method:	major credit cards
Reservations:	not accepted
Dress:	casual
Gratuity:	not included
Bar:	yes
Alcohol:	yes
Diet/light menu:	steamed and broiled items
Children's menu:	sandwiches: grilled cheese, peanut butter and jelly
Average price for meal:	$10.00
Discounts:	none offered
Catering:	yes
House favorites:	crispy flounder
Other:	Customers can order from menu of Aaron's Deli next door (HOURS: 7AM–11PM).

Have you ever been in this situation? You are going out to eat with a friend and the two of you can't agree on where to go. When Charlestonians run into this problem, they head to Hyman's Seafood Company, where you can order from not just one menu but two.

If you've visited downtown Charleston, you probably passed the old warehouse on Meeting Street, near the Omni Hotel and the Market, that houses Hyman's.

Hyman's Seafood is situated beside another restaurant, Aaron's Deli. These two places aren't just close in location. There is a special bond between their owners.

Aaron opened his deli eleven years ago and Eli his seafood place two years later. The two men are brothers. And they allow customers to order off the menu of either restaurant.

The Hyman family has long been a part of Charleston, having come to the area in the late 1800s. The family ran a dry goods business for several generations. That changed when Aaron opened his deli. Eli soon followed suit. This was a big break for residents of the city. In Charleston, Hyman's is "where locals go to get their seafood."

It didn't take long for the two restaurants to become popular among the natives, who quickly discovered their good fortune. The close proximity of the two establishments to the Market encouraged tourist traffic and soon visitors flocked to the Hyman brothers' tables. Jennifer Asnip, a Charleston resident, says, "If you're going to Hyman's in June, July, or August, you better expect an hour and a half wait."

The draw for these restaurants is, of course, the food. Hyman's, which has been voted the number one seafood establishment in Charleston, has its seafood brought in fresh daily. In addition to the excellence of the cuisine, the prices are reasonable. "Our prices are the same all day. We don't raise the prices for dinner like most places do," said manager Frank Proietti.

It's difficult for patrons to pick a favorite item from Hyman's menu. The shrimp ($10.95), sauteed mussels ($8.95), soft shell crab dinner ($12.95), and chicken fettucine (marinara or alfredo, $13.95) are all big sellers. For those looking for a smaller meal, there is the seafood po-boy sandwiches ($7.50) and a number of homemade soups: she crab, thirteen-bean, and okra gumbo (cup, $2.95; bowl, $3.95).

If you are a fish lover, you will be in heaven at Hyman's. There are fifteen to twenty-five different kinds of fish on the menu daily, ranging in price from $5.95 to $9.95. Dishes are prepared according to your direction: broiled, fried, Cajun style, sauteed, Caribbean Jerk, or steamed.

Over at the deli you find traditional items. In fact, Aaron's is called Charleston's only true New York style deli. There's kosher hot corned beef on rye (large, $7.95; small, $5.50), kosher salami on rye (large, $7.75; small, $4.95), kosher knockwurst with sauerkraut ($3.95), lox-bagel-and-cream cheese ($5.95), and a herring platter ($5.50).

The only complaint locals have about the two restaurants is their increasing notoriety. Each is consistently mentioned in national articles written about the city. *Life* Magazine, the *New York Times*, and *Travel & Leisure* are just three of the major publications that have included write-ups on the Hyman restaurants.

The next time you're dining with a friend and you are in the mood for flounder but your companion wants pastrami on rye, head for Hyman's. Both of you will be satisfied.

The Old Post Office Restaurant

Owner or manager:	David Gressette and Philip Bardin
Address:	SC 174, Edisto Island
Directions:	Take SC 174 onto Edisto Island. (It's the only route.) After crossing Intracoastal Waterway, continue approx. 8 miles. Restaurant is on left, next door to These Hands Gift Shop, just before Store Creek. Building is white with red trim and tin roof.
Phone number:	843-869-2339
Hours of operation:	TUE–SAT 6:00–10:00PM
Payment method:	major credit cards
Reservations:	recommended
Dress:	casual
Gratuity:	15% on groups of 6 or more
Bar:	yes
Alcohol:	yes
Diet/light menu:	broiled seafood
Children's menu:	child's plate available
Average price for meal:	$18.00
Discounts:	none offered
Catering:	no
House favorites:	shrimp and grits, flounder
Other:	sister restaurant at pier

Many restaurant owners spend a considerable amount of time and energy trying to come up with just the right theme for their place. Often they pay consultants thousands of dollars to help find something that will be catchy and unique. When David Gressette and Philip Bardin decided to open up their restaurant on Edisto Island, they didn't have to go through all that. Their building already had a theme. They simply adopted it.

The island's old post office became a restaurant called The Old Post Office. Instead of coming in for mail, people now come in for a meal.

David and Philip had gone to school together, but lost touch for a few years. "I was practically raised on Edisto," David explains. "I spent all my summers here. My grandfather owned the pavilion down on the beach. In 1988 I was living in Hilton Head and was here on vacation when I ran into Philip."

At the time, Philip was head chef at Fairfield Ocean Ridge. The two began talking about the idea of opening a place of their own together. They soon set about making a plan.

In looking for a location on the island, they discovered the old post office property was available and leased it. The building had been constructed in 1880 and the partners wanted to be sure they maintained the architectectural integrity of the old place. When they began renovations they made sure the style of windows, the tin roof, and other details were in keeping with the original design.

"This used to be where people gathered," David said, telling about the old combination general store and post office. "The postmaster delivered the mail on horseback. He later used a Model A."

David bought the original post office boxes and had them installed in the entrance to the restaurant along with the window where stamps were sold. Outside, he has several mail boxes (as decoration). "The Post Office didn't mind me buying them but asked me to weld them shut so people wouldn't drop letters in them," he said.

The decor, however, takes a back seat to the food. The seafood and vegetables are always fresh. While Philip stays in the kitchen, David is out running around, picking out the best food available. "Seafood and vegetable places know to call me when they get something especially nice," David said.

Philip bakes fresh bread each day and makes all desserts on the premises. David calls his partner "very creative in the kitchen." The menu is testimony to that fact: pork tenderloin medallions marinated in mustard, herbs, honey, and Jack Daniel's whiskey cream sauce ($19.00); baked grouper topped with crab, spinach, peppers, and cheddar cheese, drizzled with hollandaise ($20.00); and chicken coated in pecans, topped with blueberry sauce ($17.00).

Despite The Old Post Office's exotic dishes, David and Philip are most proud of their grits. "There's not a plate that goes out of the kitchen that doesn't have grits on it," David said. In fact, grits has become so popular the partners now sell the organic, whole grain in two-pound bags ($5.00) under their own label.

People arrive at the restaurant in everything from limousines (out of Charleston) to the old family car (from the cottages along the beach). Some even come by boat (a staff member from the restaurant will pick you up at the pier, then return you after dinner). If you'd like to eat on the water, you can eat at The Old Post Office's sister restaurant, the Sunset Grill, on the pier.

Rest assured, this is one post office where you are always happy with what is delivered.

Pinckney Cafe
and Espresso

Owner or manager:	Scott Fales
Address:	18 Pinckney Street, Charleston
Directions:	Pinckney Street (2 blocks N of Market) runs the short distance from Meeting Street to East Bay. The restaurant sits at the corner of Motley Lane, one block from East Bay.
Phone number:	843-577-0961
Hours of operation:	TUE–THU 11:30AM–3:00PM, 6:00–10PM FRI–SAT 11:00AM–10:00PM
Payment method:	cash only
Reservations:	recommended for groups of 6 or more
Dress:	casual
Gratuity:	not included
Bar:	no
Alcohol:	beer and wine
Diet/light menu:	salads, grilled items
Children's menu:	grilled cheese sandwich
Average price for meal:	$7.00, lunch • $14.00, dinner
Discounts:	none offered
Catering:	no
House favorites:	black bean burrito, seafood gumbo

Downtown Charleston has become so populated with visitors it is rare to find a restaurant that is not constantly packed with out-of-towners. There are still a few places, however, that remain hidden from the masses.

Located in the heart of downtown, the Pinckney Cafe isn't one you are going to stumble across unless you are looking for it. The street the restaurant is named for is small and secluded, tucked away between Meeting and East Bay. The cafe occupies a single house (one of those long, narrow houses with the skinny end facing the street, typical of Charleston architecture) on Pinckney Street.

Inside, the counter separates you from the kitchen. Don't sit down and wait for a waitress to bring you a fancy menu.

The menu is handwritten on a blackboard over the counter. You place your order, sit at a table in the dining area or on the long porch, and wait for the food to be brought out.

Each room has a fireplace and original pine floors. The walls are smartly decorated with work by local artists. The atmosphere is delightful—and just what you'd expect in the old port city.

The Pinckney Cafe is owned by Scott Fales. "I had been in the restaurant business for five years when this place came on the market in 1985. My wife and I jumped at the opportunity to buy it," he says.

The building had been used as a restaurant previously, but it was sitting empty when the couple decided to purchase it. After some renovation, it re-opened as Pinckney Cafe.

"I do the cooking," Scott says. "My mother didn't have any daughters so she taught me to cook." My guess is Scott's cooking has evolved from what his mother taught him. Compared to the standard fare found on most family dining tables, Scott's dishes might be called "fancy." His filet mignon is encrusted with black pepper and covered with a brandy and cream sauce ($15.99). His grilled duck breast is served with a muscadine grape sauce ($12.99). Other dinner selections are equally elaborate. The lunch fare, however, is simpler: grilled dolphin ($7.99), chicken burrito ($6.99), and omelets ($5.99).

Desserts are a big thing at the Pinckney Cafe. They change daily, as do all menu items, but can include such offerings as old-fashioned chocolate cake, bread pudding with bourbon hard sauce, peach cobbler, and turtle cheesecake. The specialty coffees are another favorite at this restaurant. Cappuccino, espresso, cafe Borgia, cafe au lait, or ciccoloccina gives a nice finishing touch to any meal.

If you're looking for great food without having a great hassle with the crowd, the Pinckney Cafe is an oasis in a desert of tourists.

SeeWee Restaurant

Owner or manager:	Mary Rancourt
Address:	4804 US 17 N, Awendaw
Directions:	From Charleston, follow US 17 N. Restaurant is 8.3 miles past Boone Hall Plantation, on left side of highway.
Phone number:	843-928-3609
Hours of operation:	MON–THU 11:00AM–9:00PM, SAT 7:30AM–10:00PM, SUN 11:00AM–3:00PM
Payment method:	major credit cards
Reservations:	not needed
Dress:	casual
Gratuity:	not included
Bar:	no
Alcohol:	beer and wine
Diet/light menu:	grilled chicken, seafood
Children's menu:	child's plate available
Average price for meal:	$5.00, lunch • $11.00, dinner
Discounts:	none offered
Catering:	yes
House favorites:	fried shrimp
Other:	take-out available

For years, the small community of Awendaw in Charleston County had a successful general store called the SeeWee. Though no longer a general store, the SeeWee is still going strong—as a restaurant.

Mary Rancourt, the owner, explains how this transition occurred: "This place was built in the 1920s as a general store. My husband and I bought it from the original owners in the 1960s and continued running it in this manner."

When Mary's husband died four years ago, she began to look for something new to do. She decided to turn the store into a restaurant. "My father had a restaurant when I was a teenager and I worked in it," she said.

Members of Mary's family came forward to help her in

her new enterprise. Several are in the seafood business them-selves and they make sure she gets the freshest shrimp, crabs, and fish. Her sister and sister-in-law contribute by baking a variety of desserts each day, one of SeeWee's specialties.

"People can buy whole cakes if they wish but they do need to give us a day's notice," Mary said. "Just a couple of days ago the phone rang. When I answered it, a man re-sponded with two words: 'Coconut cake.'"

' The atmosphere is very much that of an old-timey general store. The walls and shelves are filled with clay jugs, kerosene lanterns, duck decoys, faded photographs, old bottles, and even parts of a whiskey still.

While the decor is intriguing, the best part is the food. The SeeWee doesn't try to be exotic or fancy, and you can forget about watching your calories and cholesterol while there. Much of the cooking is done by Barry Wilson, who is also in charge of most of SeeWee's catering.

Frying is the big thing at the restaurant. You can get din-ners of fried shrimp ($10.95), fried scallops ($11.95), and fried oysters ($11.95). Steaks and chicken are available for non-sea-food eaters.

Some visitors are surprised that their meals don't come

with the traditional salad and potato. Instead, there is a complete vegetable list. You can pick from fried eggplant, fried squash, fried green tomatoes, macaroni and cheese, collard greens, rice and gravy, red rice, and an irresistible sweet potato casserole.

For lunch there are sandwiches, such as barbecue ($3.25), hamburger ($3.25), and chicken breast ($3.75). There are also seafood baskets with fries and slaw: shrimp ($8.95), oyster ($8.95), whiting ($8.95), and soft-shelled crab ($9.95).

Many people wonder how the SeeWee got its name. According to Mary, it comes from the Indian tribe that once lived in the area. It's doubtful, however, if the Indians ever ate this good.

♦ The Cooper River Bridge Run attracts thousands of runners and walkers to Charleston each April.

Olde House Cafe

Owner or manager:	Tim and Donna Sumner
Address:	920 Bells Hwy. (SC 64), Walterboro
Directions:	From I-95, take SC 64 (exit 57) SE toward Walterboro. Restaurant is less than a mile from I-95, on left side of highway.
Phone number:	843-538-2614
Hours of operation:	7 DAYS A WEEK 6:30AM–9:00PM
Payment method:	local checks
Reservations:	not needed
Dress:	casual
Gratuity:	not included
Bar:	no
Alcohol:	not served
Diet/light menu:	salad bar
Children's menu:	hot dogs, chicken fingers
Average price for meal:	buffet, $7.00
Discounts:	none offered
Catering:	yes
House favorites:	everything on the buffet

Many restaurants brag that they know who their customers are. When you go to the Olde House Cafe in Walterboro for the first time, owner Tim Sumner will know.

Tim runs the restaurant, assisted by members of his family. He is proud to point out that he's familiar with his clientele. "Between me, my wife, and my sister, we can call ninety percent of our customers by their first name." Customers like the fact that a family member is always on the premises. Tim, his wife Donna, and his sister Linda Butler rotate hours so that someone can always be there to take care of any problems.

Patrons of Old House Cafe come from varied walks of life. Commuters stop on their way to work for breakfast. Employees of nearby businesses walk over for lunch. Entire families come in for dinner. The attraction for all these people is the same: the food. "Everything we serve is made from scratch. We don't buy any pre-cooked food," Tim says.

Tim didn't grow up in the restaurant business. "I was in the construction business," he explains. "I built a restaurant for some friends. After that, my wife and I got the idea that maybe we might want to own a restaurant ourselves."

About that time, Olde House Cafe came on the market. Its owners were retiring and Tim and Donna jumped at the opportunity to purchase it. "I had never run a restaurant before, but there's nothing more to it than running any other kind of business," Tim said. "Also, we were fortunate because just about all the employees stayed with us."

The restaurant's claim to fame is down-home, country cooking. The dinner buffet includes three meats, a variety of vegetables, the salad and dessert bar, and tea or coffee for $7.00 ($5.80 at lunch). "The buffet changes every night," Linda said. "Wednesday is real popular. We have pork pileau, beef stew, and fried chicken."

In addition to the buffet, there is a menu. For seafood lovers there is fried shrimp ($11.25), deviled crab ($8.00), fried or grilled scallops ($11.25), tuna steak ($11.00), and a combination platter of fish, deviled crab, shrimp, oysters, and scallops ($13.50). Non-seafood lovers can choose from ribeye steak ($10.00), pork chops ($8.00), and grilled chicken breast ($8.00).

There is also a variety of sandwiches, such as hot dogs ($1.25) and grilled chicken croissant ($4.50). To go along with that sandwich, you can order sweet potato fries ($1.00), blooming onion ($4.00), or batter fried mushrooms ($2.50).

The locals know about Olde House Cafe through word of mouth, according to Linda. The restaurant also draws customers from nearby I-95. "I'm surprised at the number of people who keep a log of where they eat. Then when they're in the vicinity again, they come back," she said.

When you visit Olde House Cafe, be sure to introduce yourself. Maybe soon you too will be on a first-name basis.

Eva's Restaurant

Owner or manager:	Eva Hinson and Betty Davis
Address:	129 S. Main Street, Summerville
Directions:	From I-26, take US 17A (exit 199) toward Summerville. Follow US 17A (Main Street) downtown, about 1 mile. Restaurant is on left between Doty Street and Richardson Avenue.
Phone number:	843-873-5081
Hours of operation:	MON–FRI 7:00AM–7:00PM
Payment method:	local checks
Reservations:	not needed
Dress:	casual
Gratuity:	not included
Bar:	no
Alcohol:	beer and wine
Diet/light menu:	baked chicken
Children's menu:	child's plate available
Average price for meal:	$4.50
Discounts:	none offered
Catering:	no
House favorites:	salmon croquettes, baked chicken with dressing

A lot of things have changed since Eva Hinson went into the restaurant business fifty-five years ago. Then, there were no dishwashers, microwaves, or other modern conveniences.

Some things, however, have not changed. Eva is still peeling potatoes, shelling peas, and cutting collards. "A television crew came by the other day to take pictures of me peeling potatoes," Eva said with a laugh.

Eva's daughter, Betty Davis, helps run the restaurant. "Everyone, as they check out, takes a peek at mother in her rocking chair back in the kitchen, preparing fresh vegetables," Betty said.

Eva and her husband opened their first restaurant,

Eddie's, in September 1944. "I ended up running it because he had other interests. He liked to hunt and fish and I liked operating the business," she said. According to Eva, those were hectic times. "We stayed open until 4:00 AM. That's when the shift changed at the Navy yard," she recalls.

After Eddie's closed, Eva stayed out of the restaurant business just nine months. In 1953, she launched Eva's. "We used to be open seven days a week and I was working from first light to dark. Then I cut out Sundays and then Saturdays. Now we're open just weekdays. That's enough," Eva said.

Eva arrives at 6:00 AM. and starts breakfast. She also does some of the baking. "I make the pies. Coconut is one of our customers' favorites. And I sometimes make bread pudding; everyone likes that." Eva departs around 2:00 or 3:00, about the time Betty arrives. Betty stays until closing.

There are daily specials ($4.50), such as baked chicken and dressing, fried pork tenderloin, and grilled hamburger steak and onions. The specials are served with three vegetables (your choice). You can also order from the menu: sandwiches ($1.50 to $3.00) or meals (such as half a fried chicken, $6.00).

The restaurant is located in the heart of Summerville's business district, next door to an interesting antique shop, so you can combine eating a meal with shopping. The location makes it convenient for downtown merchants and other workers to drop in for breakfast or lunch. "Some of our customers actually eat here twice a day," Betty said. "There are people who have been coming here since we opened."

Customers aren't the only ones who love Eva's. "I've worked here for twenty-seven years," said waitress Eunice Rogers. "I really enjoy it."

The decor of the restaurant features Eva's collection of state plates. "I got them at a jewelry store. In this business, I've never been able to travel enough to collect them myself," Eva said. There are forty-eight plates in the collection. Montana and Louisiana were knocked off the wall and broken, so Eva is on the look-out for replacements.

Flo's Place

Owner or manager:	Flo and Ralph Triska
Address:	US 17BUS, Murrells Inlet
Directions:	From Myrtle Beach, follow US 17BUS S, past Surfside and Garden City Beaches, to Murrells Inlet (about 13 miles). US 17BUS runs through Murrells Inlet (about 4 miles). Restaurant is on left (ocean) side of highway, in the middle of Murrells Inlet.
Phone number:	843-651-7222
Hours of operation:	7 DAYS A WEEK 11:30AM–10:00PM
Payment method:	checks, major credit cards
Reservations:	not needed
Dress:	casual
Gratuity:	not included
Bar:	yes
Alcohol:	yes
Diet/light menu:	no
Children's menu:	yes
Average price for meal:	$5.00–$7.00, lunch • $12.00–$20.00, dinner
Discounts:	none offered
Catering:	no
House favorites:	The Dunkin Pot, shrimp creole, alligator stew

If you're looking for a great restaurant in which to hang your hat, try Flo's Place. Of course, you might have a problem finding a space, since over 3,000 hats already hang on every available surface in the place.

It is not the amazing hat collection, though, that draws people to Flo's. It is the great atmosphere and the even greater food that brings in the steady stream of locals and tourists.

Since opening eighteen years ago, Flo's has been owned and operated by Flo and Ralph Triska. Guests are greeted by Flo, who looks elegant in a vintage dress and handsome hat.

"I have clothes that go back to the 1920s in my closet at home," she says with pride.

The restaurant is a family affair. "Our daughter is the manager, my husband is the brains, and I'm the BS artist," Flo said with a laugh.

The restaurant seats 120 people. That figure includes the tables on the covered porch, overlooking the marsh. Ceiling fans and ocean breezes keep the porch comfortable.

As for the food, it's Cajun. "I'm from New Orleans and these are all my mother's recipes," Flo says.

Individuals who have never had real Cajun food are in for a treat. One of the house specialties is alligator stew. The recipe starts with roux to which is added sauteed strips of alligator meat, fish stock, sausage, onions, celery, tomatoes, and ten different spices. The dish is served in a miniature cast-iron kettle and priced at $4.00. Another favorite is fried ocean perch, served with fries and slaw. The fish is dusted with Cajun seasonings and not at all greasy. The large portion is only $5.95. Dinner specials include seafood gumbo ($12.95), red beans and rice with sausage ($11.95), and blackened fish ($14.95).

"It's hard to find good Cajun food anymore, even in New Orleans," Ralph said. "We make everything fresh. The philosophy behind our cooking is to take any favorite Cajun recipe and do it the best it can be done."

According to Ralph, Flo's Place was the first restaurant in South Carolina to serve Cajun food, the first to prepare blackened fish, and the first to offer alligator meat. "We serve more alligator meat than anyone else in the state," he said. In addition to the stew, they serve alligator ribs and alligator fritters.

For those not partial to Cajun food, there is the Henry the Eighth ribeye ($18.95), New England lobster ($19.95), and a number of seafood platters. There is also a children's menu. And the kids receive Mardi Gras beads as a souvenir.

Next time you're on the Grand Strand, make sure to head to Flo's Place for some good food—and remember to bring your hat.

Rice Paddy

Owner or manager:	Susan Felder and Susan Hibbs
Address:	819 Front Street, Georgetown
Directions:	From US 17, take Broad Street S, toward the water. Follow Broad until it runs into Front Street. Turn right onto Front. Restaurant is in the first block on the right.
Phone number:	843-546-2021
Hours of operation:	MON–SAT 11:30AM–2:30PM, 6:00–10:00PM
Payment method:	major credit cards
Reservations:	recommended in summer
Dress:	nice casual
Gratuity:	not included
Bar:	no
Alcohol:	beer and wine
Diet/light menu:	salads, broiled seafood, chicken
Children's menu:	no
Average price for meal:	$6.00, lunch • $15.00–$20.00, dinner
Discounts:	none offered
Catering:	yes
House favorites:	rack of lamb, crab cakes, Bahamian grouper

When Susan Hibbs and Susan Felder were working at Pawley's Island Inn, they probably never dreamed they'd end up owning one of Georgetown's most successful restaurants.

"We had been at Pawley's Island awhile when we had a chance to buy a little place in Georgetown," Susan Hibbs said.

The "little place" was a tea room that served soup and sandwiches and was open only for lunch. The two friends set to work, adding menu items and evening hours. That was thirteen years ago. Back then, both women cooked and performed any of the other tasks that needed to be done.

"We built up our reputations. People got to know us and eventually we needed a bigger place," Susan Hibbs said. Today, the Rice Paddy's forty employees work shifts to keep the business running smoothly.

"Now I'm in the kitchen and Susan works out front," Susan Felder said. "I've always been the one more interested in food. I learned to cook from my father and grandfather. Food was always an important part of our family life."

Susan Felder said her aim at the Rice Paddy is to serve food like you eat at home, prepared with care and love. "We vary our menu depending on what's in season. We try to use local things. If we can't get it fresh, we don't serve it," she said. Susan Felder prepares lunch and bakes the desserts. There's another chef for the evening meal. "He's a fellow who worked with us at Pawley's Island," she said. "He went on to a couple of other places and we finally talked him into coming to the Rice Paddy." The two chefs work out the menu together. "We try to have a representative from each meat group," the lunch chef said. "We also consider our customers' input. People request certain items. That's fine with us because we like to try new things."

Some of the favorite dining menu items of the locals are

roast rack of lamb moutarde, pan roasted snapper with wild mushrooms and leeks, Bahamian grouper, and crab cakes. Among seasonal specialties are deep fried soft-shell crabs and bacon-wrapped shad roe. The price range is upscale but well worth the money. Examples from the menu are veal scallopini with roasted red pepper and goat cheese sauce ($19.95), pan fried quail with country ham cream gravy and grits ($17.95), snapper piccata ($16.95), grilled pork tenderloin with maple glaze ($15.95).

Lunch is equally varied but much lower in price. Sandwiches include open-faced hot crab ($6.95); smoked turkey on wheat with avocado and sprouts ($5.95); and grilled eggplant, zucchini, onion, red pepper, and goat cheese on a bataard ($7.95). All are served with homemade chips. Salads include shrimp, chicken, pasta, and tuna ($5.95–$8.95). There are also specialties, such as shrimp, bacon, and spinach quesadilla ($6.95); grilled grouper with capers, black olives, and sun-dried tomatoes served with baked orzo ($9.95); and crab enchiladas with green chile sauce ($7.95).

With such an outstanding menu, a visit the Rice Paddy will make any beach trip a memorable one.

River Room

Owner or manager:	Sid Hood and Sally Swineford
Address:	801 Front Street, Georgetown
Directions:	From US 17, take Broad Street S, toward the water. Follow Broad until it ends at Front Street. Restaurant is on the boardwalk, where Broad and Front meet.
Phone number:	843-527-4110
Hours of operation:	MON–SAT 11:00AM–2:30PM, 5:00–10:00PM
Payment method:	major credit cards
Reservations:	not accepted
Dress:	casual
Gratuity:	not included
Bar:	yes
Alcohol:	yes
Diet/light menu:	grilled dishes
Children's menu:	yes
Average price for meal:	$5.00, lunch • $15.00, dinner
Discounts:	none offered
Catering:	no
House favorites:	grilled seafood

When Sid Hood decided to open a restaurant, he bought an old building in downtown Georgetown and began renovations. Two and a half years and twenty-eight permits later, River Room was born.

"I had had one foot in the restaurant business for a long time and was a partner in a couple of places," he said, adding that his primary occupation was that of ship's captain. He delivered boats up and down the Intracoastal Waterway. That's when he became aware of Georgetown.

When Sid and his partner, Sally Swineford, opened their restaurant fifteen years ago, Georgetown had not yet renovated its downtown. Today, Front Street is a delightfully quaint area in the historic section featuring a tremendous boardwalk and a variety of unique and interesting shops. Sid's restaurant fits right in. The windows of River Room provide a gorgeous view of the Sampit River—and Sid's boat anchored right off the boardwalk.

The original building, which dates back more than a century, was once home to two old businesses, a grocery store and a dry goods store. When Sid was fixing up the second floor of the restaurant, he tore up the old linoleum. Beneath, used as insulation, were copies of the *New York Times* from the 1800s.

Sid framed one page of the paper to hang downstairs along with photographs of old Georgetown. "The pictures were taken by a man named Morgan. He was mayor at the turn of the century and quite a photographer," Sid said. The Georgetown Library Museum has a complete collection of Morgan's work, and there is a published book of his photographs.

River Room has a standard menu plus specials that change daily. Dinners include petit filet and sautéed shrimp ($19.95), shrimp and scallop tasso ($13.95), grilled tuna ($15.95) and Joe's Stuffed Chicken ($13.95). For an appetizer you might select shrimp and grits ($5.95), spicy fried calamari ($5.95), or McClellanville Lump Crab Cakes ($6.95).

Possible lunch choices are Cajun stuffed chicken ($5.95), sweet and sour chicken fettucine ($5.95), shepherd's pie ($4.95), salmon cakes ($5.95), and cold boiled shrimp ($5.95). You might want to try the shrimp and grits, a meal in itself at midday, an appetizer in the evening, and the name of Sid's boat. The menu also includes a variety of salads.

The desserts are truly delicious. In fact, the sautéed pound cake won first place in a culinary competition. "It's just like it sounds," Sid said. "We sauté a slice of pound cake. Then we serve it in a pool of caramel sauce." Other special desserts include sweet potato pie (made from scratch) and Brownie Points with praline ice cream and fresh strawberry sauce. On the menu are peanut butter pie, mud pie, key lime pie, and German chocolate cheesecake. All desserts are $3.50 each.

♦ Georgetown is the third oldest city in the state.

Alice's Café

Owner or manager:	Alice Cannon
Address:	5835 Dick Pond Road, Socastee
Directions:	From US 17 (about 6.5 miles below Myrtle Beach pavilion), take SC 544 NW 2.7 miles to Socastee (SC 707). Cross SC 707 and take first right past high school (Dick Pond Road). Restaurant is about 2 miles on left, beside bridge.
Phone number:	843-215-3392
Hours of operation:	MON–THU 6:00AM–2:00PM; FRI 6:00AM–2:00PM, 6:00–9:00PM; SAT 7:00AM–12:00N
Payment method:	cash only
Reservations:	not needed
Dress:	casual
Gratuity:	not included
Bar:	no
Alcohol:	not served
Diet/light menu:	chicken dishes
Children's menu:	yes
Average price for meal:	$3.50, breakfast • $5.00, lunch • $7.50, dinner
Discounts:	none offered
Catering:	no
House favorites:	chicken and dumplings, hamburgers

Some restaurant owners like to discuss how difficult it is to own and run their businesses. After hearing them run on for some time, you might start to wonder if performing brain surgery might be easier than being in the restaurant business. But you won't ever hear talk like that from Alice Cannon. Alice had worked as a waitress but had never run a restaurant before opening her own place, Alice's Café.

So what made her think she could do it? "You want to know the truth?" she asked. "You only have to know two things to run a restaurant: how to buy groceries and how to pay bills."

It made sense for Alice to go into the restaurant business. She had always loved to cook and liked having people enjoy what she prepared, so owning a place seemed ideal.

A few years ago she decided to open a small diner across from the high school in Socastee, a small inland town just north of Surfside Beach. "People began coming," Alice said, "and pretty soon they were having to wait to get a table. I knew they didn't have time to be standing around so I decided to get a bigger place." Alice's Café moved to Brant's Landing on the Intracoastal Waterway, beside the swing bridge (one of only two such bridges left on the Waterway). When asked if the bridge ever swings to open, one of the waitresses said, "All the time, especially when I'm hurrying trying to get to work."

The cafe has a friendly feel and the decor is definitely country. You know you're in a place where locals eat because the waitresses are heard to ask, "Your usual?"

Alice runs the place with help from her family. Daughter Crystal Bell works full-time as a waitress. "My mom's a great cook," Crystal said. "She's been cooking since she was nine. She's from a big family so she learned how to cook real young." Alice's son is backup cook and her sister is cashier.

Breakfast at the cafe consists of two eggs, grits or hash browns, bacon or sausage, and a biscuit or toast ($2.50.) Add two pancakes for only $1.00 more and you will be filled for the day.

The daily lunch special includes one meat, three vegetables, a biscuit or cornbread, tea, and dessert ($4.89). One of the restaurant's most popular items is its old-fashioned hamburger ($3.25). "We use fresh ground beef and patty it out ourselves," Alice said. "It takes about fifteen to twenty minutes to cook one; they're that big. When people order them, we warn them it will take awhile." (In other words, these are no fast-food hamburgers.) The homemade chili served on hot dogs and hamburgers at Alice's Café is popular too. "That really makes a great hamburger," the owner adds. Besides the terrific hamburgers, sandwiches include grilled bologna and cheese, grilled ham, pork chop, and BLT ($2.00–$3.25).

Dinner choices include fried oysters ($7.95), fried flounder ($6.95), New York strip ($9.95), and fried chicken ($4.95).

With the skill she has in preparing food, it's no wonder Alice thinks running a restaurant isn't too difficult. Lucky for her customers she is so good at the job.

♦ In the summer of 1901, E. G. Burroughs of Conway opened Myrtle Beach's first hotel, the Seaside Inn.

♦ The Grand Strand officially begins at Winyah Bay (at the city of Georgetown) in the old rice plantation country and runs northeast sixty miles to Little River Neck.

Boots' and John's Biscuit Shack

Owner or manager:	Boots Jordan
Address:	Sea Mountain Hwy., Cherry Grove
Directions:	From Myrtle Beach pavilion, follow US 17 N about 18 miles to SC 9. Turn right onto SC 9 (toward beach); go one block to Sea Mountain Hwy. Turn right onto Sea Mountain; go 3/10 mile. Restaurant on left.
Phone number:	843-249-3224
Hours of operation:	7 DAYS A WEEK 5:00AM–9:30PM
Payment method:	checks
Reservations:	not needed
Dress:	casual
Gratuity:	not included
Bar:	no
Alcohol:	not served
Diet/light menu:	chicken dishes
Children's menu:	yes
Average price for meal:	$6.00 to $10.00
Discounts:	none offered
Catering:	no
House favorites:	oyster platter, chicken
Other:	good desserts for only $1.00

Whenever Boots Jordan sets to work on something, she doesn't waste much time. There can be no clearer example of this than the way she handled the move of her restaurant to its new location. "The new Biscuit Shack is right behind where my old place was," she said. "When I moved, I closed the old place at 9:00 PM and opened the new one at 5:00 the next morning." By noon, she had knocked the old building down. "Of course, it didn't take much. One shove and it was gone," she said.

Boots has been running the Biscuit Shack for the last twenty years. But she hadn't always been in the restaurant business. "Until then, I had spent my whole life in retail," she says. "When I decided to get out of that, I needed something else to do. I had been coming to the beach for about twenty years. The next time I came, I said, I wasn't going home."

Boots stood by her word. On her next visit to the Grand Strand, she decided to stay and open a restaurant. She bought a lot in North Myrtle Beach at the corner of what is now Sea Mountain Highway and Hill Street. At the time there wasn't anything else around. Of course, today it is a prime location.

Boots purchased the business, already named Biscuit Shack, from Robert Platt. "I decided to keep the name, though sometimes they call me the Roll Shack when I run out of biscuits," she jokes. Boots ran the restaurant in the tiny shack until she could afford to build the new, larger building. "That's the way I do things: I wait until I can afford it," she said.

Boots' and John's Biscuit Shack is open from 5:00 AM to 10:00 PM, seven days a week. Because of the long hours, Boots runs two shifts of employees. But she is there whenever the restaurant is open. "I haven't had a vacation—not even a day off— in eleven years," she says. She means this quite literally. Believe it or not, she even opens Christmas morning. "On that day," she says, "I use only employees who volunteer. There are some who want to work then. It's more relaxed—a jovial time to work."

While the restaurant gets its share of tourists in the summer, the locals make up the majority of the clientelle during cooler months. There are, however, a number of northern *snowbirds* who come South during the winter. With a keen knowledge of her customers, Boots can quickly scan the restaurant and tell you exactly who are locals and who are not.

The food is good and plentiful. The large oyster platter ($7.95) has twenty-five oysters (small platter, $6.95). There is also stuffed flounder ($8.95), half a chicken ($5.10), and seafood platters (large, $9.95; small, $6.95). Sandwiches are served too ($1.50 to $3.00). The biggest bargain is the daily special: one of three choices of meat and three of a list of vegetables (lunch, $3.72; dinner, $4.00; child's plate, $2.33). Homemade cakes (pineapple, chocolate, and coconut) and pies (Boston creme and chocolate ice box) are $1.00 per slice.

Grandma's Kitchen

Owner or manager:	Richard and Janice Selvey
Address:	US 17 at 7th Ave. S, Myrtle Beach
Directions:	Downtown Mytle Beach, corner of US 17 and 7th Ave. S.
Phone number:	843-448-2126
Hours of operation:	7 DAYS A WEEK 7:00AM–10:00PM
Payment method:	major credit cards
Reservations:	not needed
Dress:	casual
Gratuity:	not included
Bar:	no
Alcohol:	not served
Diet/light menu:	salad bar
Children's menu:	yes
Average price for meal:	$5.50, lunch buffet • $11.95, dinner buffet
Discounts:	none offered
Catering:	no
House favorites:	fried chicken, homemade desserts

When Richard and Janice Selvey named their restaurant Grandma's Kitchen, they weren't trying to be trendy or cute. They were referring to a real grandma. "My husband's grandmother," Janice explains, "had a restaurant called Annie's. Many old-timers in Myrtle Beach still remember it. Annie was said to be quite a cook. According to family legend, she was offered a lot of money by Betty Crocker for her pancake recipe but wouldn't sell. We still use her recipe in our restaurant. In fact, many things we fix are from her recipes."

Richard served in the military before he and Janice moved back to Myrtle Beach. He dabbled in insurance for a time and then ran a roofing company. Like his grandmother Annie and his father, who owned the restaurant Village Idiot, Richard eventually got into the food business. The Selveys started with a little coffee shop, then leased (and later bought) the lot at the corner of 7th Avenue and US 17.

The Selveys are antique buffs and use their restaurant to display their collection of authentic advertising signs. At the rear of the dining room is a replica of an 1800s barbershop complete with a banjo playing customer. "We built this building," Janice said of the quaint, homey restaurant. "We've enlarged the building once and remodeled a couple of times."

The success of the restaurant can be traced to the talent of the Selveys' employees and the love and support of family. There are the two cooks. Sonny's been with them since they opened. Willie's employment goes back about sixteen years. Presently, two of their three daughters work at the restaurant and a twenty-year old granddaughter is there during summers and on weekends. "We've all been raised in here," said youngest daughter Tammy Thompson. "My daughter is only ten but she can run the register or help in the kitchen."

Much of the restaurant's business is from local folks—city employees, police officers, and businessmen—but, because of its location, Grandma's Kitchen is easy for tourists to find. "A lot of people tell me they eat here whenever they come to the beach," Janice said. Judy Johnson, a surgical nurse, is a frequent customer. "I eat here several times a week," she said. "The buffet is fantastic. The desserts are really delicious."

Janice or one of the cooks bakes the pies, cobblers, biscuits, and cornbread on the premises. Chicken is a specialty—no one will tell what makes it so different. Vegetables are fresh and cooked in imaginative ways—the cauliflower is a real treat. The lunch buffet, which includes the salad and dessert bars, is $5.50. The evening seafood and country buffet, with salad and dessert bars, is $11.95. You can also order meals (average, $10.00) or sandwiches (average, $4.00) off the menu.

Grandma's is open every day of the year. "Christmas is one of our busiest days," Janice said. "We have people who get off I-95 to have Thanksgiving or Christmas dinner with us."

If the real grandma was still around, she'd be proud to eat at Grandma's Kitchen.

Mr. Fish

Owner or manager:	Ted Hammerman
Address:	919 Broadway, Myrtle Beach
Directions:	From US 501 at US 17, take US 501 E (toward the ocean) about 1-1/2 miles to Broadway (1 block before US 17BUS). Left onto Broadway, go about 2-1/2 blocks. Restaurant on left between 9th and 10th Ave. N, adjacent to city hall, across from United Methodist church.
Phone number:	843-946-6869
Hours of operation:	MON–TUE 11:00AM–3:30PM, WED–FRI 11:00AM–5:00PM, SAT 5:00–9:30PM
Payment method:	major credit cards
Reservations:	not needed
Dress:	casual
Gratuity:	not included
Bar:	no
Alcohol:	beer, wine, and sake
Diet/light menu:	seafood
Children's menu:	no
Average price for meal:	$7.00
Discounts:	none offered
Catering:	yes
House favorites:	fish sandwiches
Other:	web site: www.mrfish.com

Ted Hammerman, owner of the restaurant named Mr. Fish, could reasonably be called Mr. Fish himself. Ted is an expert on fish—catching, cutting, cooking, and anything else you can do with fish.

"I got into this because I invented a fish trap. My gear was very unique. Instead of bait, it used mirrors, beads, broken glass, light sticks—those sorts of things," he said. In 1982 Ted went to India for the United Nations to teach the use of his fishing gear. "My trap was made of steel but those poor guys over there couldn't afford that so we made the traps out of bamboo or chicken wire," he said.

When Ted came back to the United States, he went into the fish wholesale business. He bought from boats coming into port and sold the cleaned and deboned fish to restaurants. All this was done from a location in Myrtle Beach that was the original 1950s seafood market (not a first-class location at the time). Myrtle Beach's popularity exploded, however, and downtown real estate became home to high-rise, luxury hotels. And there was Ted with all this seafood in the middle of it.

It dawned on him that he could convert part of the whole-sale market into a restaurant. Suddenly, he had a winner. Mr. Fish is no foo-foo place with fine china and silver. It's Styrofoam plates and plastic forks. Instead of linen-draped tables, customers sit at a counter. But, no one complains. The seafood is absolutely fresh and cooked to the customer's specifications.

Locals gather around the counter at lunch to read the paper, visit with friends, and eat a fresh fish sandwich. "We can fry, blacken, jerk, grill, steam, or sauté. At Mr. Fish, you *can* have it your way," Ted said. "You can eat it here or take it with you. We have nothing to hide. Pick out the seafood you like and we'll cook it or pack it to travel."

Mr. Fish offers a daily special ($4.95), fish and chips ($4.95), salmon ($6.99), scallops ($6.99), crab cake ($6.99), oysters ($6.99), a two-item combination plate ($7.99), and numerous other seafood dishes. Side dishes include home-cut white potato fries or sweet potato fries, green beans, garlic potatoes, gumbo, fish stew, and corn on the cob. If you are a fan of sushi, you should visit on Wednesday or Thursday night.

In addition to the restaurant and seafood wholesale business, Ted does a lot of catering. He hosts oyster roasts and shrimp boils, and his party trays are a must for any Myrtle Beach party. "And we don't do pig!" Ted proclaims.

Whether you need tips on how to catch "the big one" or you just want to eat a big one, Mr. Fish is the place for you. Ted's motto is simple: "You can't live on wishes, but you can live on fishes."

Rivertown Bistro

Owner or manager:	Cyndi and Darren Smith
Address:	111 Third Avenue, Conway
Directions:	Traveling on US 501 from Myrtle Beach, take US 501BUS downtown, approx. 4 miles, to Third Avenue. Left onto Third for 1-1/2 blocks. Restaurant is on left.
Phone number:	843-248-3733
Hours of operation:	TUE–SAT 11:30AM–2:00PM, 5:00–9:30PM
Payment method:	major credit cards
Reservations:	recommended for dinner
Dress:	nice casual
Gratuity:	not included
Bar:	no
Alcohol:	beer and wine
Diet/light menu:	salads, broiled seafood, chicken
Children's menu:	child's plate available
Average price for meal:	$6.00, lunch • $15.00, dinner
Discounts:	none offered
Catering:	yes
House favorites:	blackened dolphin on grits cake
Other:	gourmet food section, gift baskets

When Cyndi Smith married, she gained more than a husband. She got a cook as well. "We met when he was working in Charleston and I was going to school there," she said. Darren trained under outstanding chefs, so after they were married, they decided to put his culinary skills to use and open a restaurant of their own. "I'm from Conway," Cyndi said, "so we came here. This restaurant was for sale. We bought it and renamed it the Rivertown Bistro."

Darren handles the kitchen while Cyndi, who majored in finance, manages the business end. This arrangement applies not just to their restaurant but to their home life. "We recently celebrated our fifth anniversary," Cyndi said, "and someone asked me how many meals I have cooked since we've been

A LOCALS' GUIDE

married. Zero. He cooks while I clean up."

Rivertown Bistro offers a wide selection of dishes, although Darren specializes in fresh seafood. "He changes the menu about every two months," Cyndi said. "He reads a lot about foods and tries out dishes he's read about. We also travel to places like New York and Chicago where he gets ideas."

The restaurant has a second cook who makes the desserts, leaving Darren free to concentrate on entrees. Items on the dinner menu are cashew chicken with fresh vegetables and a ginger soy glaze tossed with linguine ($9.95), halibut tapenade topped with a pine nut crust and served over caramelized onions ($16.95), grilled filet of beef topped with jumbo lump crab and a cabernet cracked pepper glaze ($17.95), and sauteed veal medallions with roasted garlic sauce and portabello mushrooms ($14.95). A customer favorite is blackened dolphin on a jalapeno grit cake topped with blue crab shallot cream ($14.50).

For lunch there are all kinds of sandwiches and salads

ranging in price from $5.00 to $7.00.

There is a wide selection of appetizers: Low Country spring rolls stuffed with chicken, spinach, and spicy ham, served with honey Dijon ($4.00); blackeye pea cakes with roasted corn and roma tomato salsa, served with sour cream ($3.00); and crawfish au gratin on fried eggplant with roasted red pepper cream ($6.95).

The restaurant has a small gourmet foods retail section. They sell such items as pumpkin butter, orange ginger scone mix, and Napa Valley green chile and garlic mustard. According to Cyndi, they prepare quite a few gift baskets.

Rivertown Bistro is located downtown, so it's convenient for local business people at lunch. It's also easy for out-of-towners to find. It's a little more than a block away from the town clock.

♦ No river empties into the Atlantic Ocean along the Grand Strand, and that stretch of coastline is not spotted with coastal islands like the South Carolina coastline farther south.

Sea Captain's House

Owner or manager: David Brittain
Address: 3002 N. Ocean Blvd., Myrtle Beach
Directions: Downtown, between 4th Avenue N and 5th Avenue N.
Phone number: 843-448-8082
Hours of operation: 7 DAYS A WEEK 6:00AM–10:00PM
Payment method: cash only
Reservations: not needed
Dress: casual
Gratuity: 15% included for groups of 8 or more
Bar: no
Alcohol: beer and wine
Diet/light menu: broiled seafood, grilled chicken
Children's menu: yes
Average price for meal: $ 5.00, breakfast • $8.00, lunch • $15.00, dinner
Discounts: none offered
Catering: no
House favorites: seafood platter

The building that houses the Sea Captain's House was built in 1930 as a family beach cottage. In 1954, it was converted into a guest home. The property was sold in 1962, and plans were made to tear down the building and replace it with a high-rise hotel. A shortage of financing forced these plans to be postponed. The owners decided they would operate a restaurant in the old building for a few years, until a hotel could be built.

Twenty-five years later, that restaurant is still operating. There's no way it could be torn down now. The entire city would protest. Sea Captain's House has become a Myrtle Beach landmark. Taking it away would be like taking away the Atlantic Ocean.

The restaurant is now owned by David Brittain. Philip

Rateliff is one of its managers. "I started here twelve years ago," Philip said. "A friend called me and told me about the position. I liked the job and I liked the location, so I moved here." Philip had learned his trade under the Government Apprenticeship Program. "I served under a fellow who had worked in Paris. He was an American but he was an expert in French cooking," he said.

Philip explained that what drew him to the occupation of chef was its lack of routine. "There's always something different to do, new ideas to try," he said. "Chefs are always ready to go with the new trends but we have to wait until the customers are ready. Like when I first came here, blackened fish was already popular in metropolitan areas, but it had not caught on here. Say you have some nice mangoes, on a whim, you might make a mango sauce. Or you might have some really great swordfish. We have an herb garden right across the street. I might decide to serve swordfish with an herb sauce."

When Philip first came to the Sea Captain's House, there were two dining room managers. Today, there are three dining room managers, as well as several executive chefs, prep chefs, and other workers. "None of us work real long hours," Philip says. "We're a very family-oriented group. The owner has children. I have children. I think you need quality time off to produce quality time on the job."

Sea Captain's House overlooks the ocean, providing a spectacular view. Inside, the decor is cozy and friendly. The front room has a fireplace at either end and big, comfortable sofas and chairs—perfect for lounging with a drink while you wait for a table.

The service is first rate, but the food is the real draw. Baked shrimp in phyllo topped with Hollandaise sauce ($13.50); coastal crab broil au gratin with a tangy cheddar sauce ($15.50); and southwestern seafood pasta with spinach fettuccini, fresh tomato salsa, and grated cheese ($14.95) are just a sampling of the offerings. There are all kinds of scallop, shrimp, oyster, and fish dishes.

For the non-seafood lover, there is grilled breast of chicken in pineapple-soy marinade ($12.95), a ten-ounce ribeye topped with herb butter ($16.50), and grilled pork chops glazed with honey mustard ($13.75). There is also a variety of appetizers, soups, salads, and, of course, desserts.

Sea Captain's House is a favorite eating place for folks who live in Myrtle Beach as well as those who visit. "We used to close six weeks during the winter," Philip said. "Not anymore. Myrtle Beach has become a year-round resort."

♦ Gallivant's Ferry in Horry County is the site of South Carolina's most famous political stump meeting each election year.

♦ The state shell of South Carolina is the lettered olive.

T. Jarrett's Marker and Horn

Owner or manager:	Tony Jarrett and Larry McCrea
Address:	121 N. Longstreet St., Kingstree
Directions:	From intersection of US 52 (Longstreet Street) and SC 527 downtown Kingstree, take US 52 N (toward Lake City) about 2 miles. Restaurant is on left.
Phone number:	843-354-7555
Hours of operation:	MON–SAT 11:30AM–10:00PM
Payment method:	major credit cards
Reservations:	recommended on weekends
Dress:	casual
Gratuity:	not included
Bar:	yes
Alcohol:	yes
Diet/light menu:	salads, chicken dishes
Children's menu:	no
Average price for meal:	$8.00
Discounts:	none offered
Catering:	yes
House favorites:	all seafood dishes

When faced with adversity, some people give up. Others pull themselves up by their bootstraps and keep moving forward. When Tony Jarrett lost his wholesale distribution business to fire, he knew he couldn't sit around and do nothing.

"I employed around fifteen people, including several family members," Tony said. "I didn't have fire insurance on the place so I lost everything. I was in a purple haze for about three months trying to figure out what to do. One day I drove by this building and saw a 'for sale' sign hanging on the door. It hit me then what I should do."

The two-story brick structure that inspired Tony that day is a historic landmark in downtown Kingstree, having been a bus station at one time. It was perfect, Tony decided, for a res-

taurant. Though someone had made a failed attempt at a restaurant at this very location, Tony intended to give it a shot.
His idea became reality after meeting with Larry McCrea.

"Larry was head chef at the Florence Country Club, and
when he heard I was thinking of starting a new place, he
called me and asked if we could meet. In my mind there were
three questions I had to answer before I would commit: Does
Kingstree need it? Would it be fun for me? and Could I make
a living doing it? After the first thirty minutes of our meeting,
I knew I wanted to make a go at it."

The two formed a partnership and Kingstree residents had
a new restaurant. A casual though sophisticated dining experience was something new in Williamsburg's county seat, but
it quickly drew favor with area residents.

The exterior of the historic building is enough to peak
one's interest. Once inside, you see the decor is in keeping with
its name, as the interior is decorated with old rods and reels,
hooks, and oars. There is no main dining room but a series of
small rooms, each with a different nautical name, such as "the
river room" and "the channel room."

The restaurant's name may be a bit lengthy, but it accurately describes the house specialties: seafood ("marker" referring to fishing markers) and beef ("horn")—although Tony says he had no real reason for choosing the name. "I used to sell a medical product called Hadical," he explained. "The manufacturer said they named it this because they had to call it something. I wrote down about a hundred different possibilities for this restaurant and just picked this one."

You might expect from the looks of the place that the food would be pricey but that is not the case. "I knew going into it," Tony said, "that being in Kingstree, I couldn't charge what similar restaurants in Charleston or Columbia could charge." For those who like seafood, T. Jarrett's offers a wide selection. Shrimp ($5.95), oysters ($7.95), and crab nuggets ($8.95) are traditional items. For those who like pasta, there is shrimp linguine. If beef is your thing, the filet ($12.95) is the top seller, though many people also enjoy the ribeye ($12.95). All dinner items include a trip to the salad bar. At lunch, a buffet ($5.50) offers an assortment of meats and vegetables. Burgers and sandwiches are also served, as well as salads (blackened chicken salad, $4.95; chef's, $4.25).

With T. Jarrett's Marker and Horn in town, residents of Kingstree no longer have to travel to find a restaurant with a sophisticated flair.

Notes

Index

G

H

I

J

K

L

T

T. Jarrett's Marker and Horn 234–36
Ten Governors Cafe 122–24
Thrasher, Lloyd ("Skin") 5–7
Thrasher, Matt 5–7
Thrasher, Mike 5–7
Town & Country Restaurant 50–51
Towne House, The 8–10
Travel & Leisure 198
Trifos, Angelo and Georgia 90–92
Triska, Flo and Ralph 211–12

U

Union, city of 41–42
Union County 41–42
Unlimited Magazine 55
UPSTATE 1–48
Upton, Hilda 187–89

V

Variety Restaurant 105–07
Varos, Jimmy 105–07
Villa Luigi 32–34
Village Inn 108–10

W

Walhalla, town of 26–28
Walterboro, city of 207–80
Webb, Charles 116–18
West Columbia, city of 66–68, 72–74
Whistle Stop Cafe, The 172–74
White, Ron 184–86
Whitlark, Forest 93–95
Whitlark, Paul 93–95
Whitman, Walt 62
Whitmire, Charles 38-40

Williamsburg County 234–36
Winnsboro, town of 57–58
Winton Inn 116–18
Woodward, Robert 38–40
Woodward's Cafe 38–40

Y

Yoder, Melvin 2–4
Yoder's Dutch Kitchen 2–4
York, city of 43–45
York County 43–48

Z

Zemp, Madge 146–48

BRIAN KATONAK is an assistant solicitor in Anderson County, South Carolina. Born in Aiken, he has been a lifelong resident of the Palmetto State. Brian holds a bachelor's degree in interdisciplinary studies from the University of South Carolina (USC) at Aiken and a degree in law from USC in Columbia. Brian's hobbies include traveling and running marathons to raise money for charity. Although he has published several freelance articles, this is his first book.

LYNNE KATONAK, Brian's mother, is a reporter with the *Aiken Standard*, where she has worked for more than twenty years. In 1978 she was named South Carolina Female Journalist of the Year. When Lynne is not writing, she enjoys traveling and reading.

Notice to Readers

Mom and I are already compiling restaurants for a second volume. If you would like to recommend a place, please contact me by e-mail at **bkat@juno.com** or snail-mail **c/o Sandlapper Publishing, PO Box 730, Orangeburg, SC 29116.**

—Brian Katonak